Foreign policy of the Islamic Republic of Iran in the Middle East (1979-2017)

case study : Saudi Arabia and Syria

BEHZAD DIANSAEI

Title: Foreign policy of the Islamic Republic of Iran in the Middle East (1979-2017)

Subtitle: case study: Saudi Arabia and Syria

Author: Behzad Diansaei

Cover Design: Mohsen Rahmandoust

Publisher: American Academic Research

ISBN: 978-1947464131

Table of contents

Introduction

Urgency of the research. Foreign policy is a strategy with a series of planned actions that decision-makers of a country implement in order to pursuit the specific national interest-based goals in relation to other countries or international communities. The field of international relations is constantly changing, and the creators of this structure (the actors of international system) are also adapting to these changes. Due to the specific importance of the Middle East, changes and transformations that this region is facing nowadays influence the other countries of the world.

As you know, Iran is strategically and geopolitically one of the most important countries in the world. One of the strengths of this country is its geographic position, Iran has maritime and land boundaries with fifteen countries. After the Islamic revolution in 1979, Iran's foreign policy was largely based on Islamic values and changed its nature according to Islamic guidelines.

The Iran-Iraq war and changing most of the former allies have also influenced the foreign policy, by shifting it to the most intense one. Some believe that Iran's over-representation in the region and in particular, the Arab Middle East faces unnecessary challenges and therefore brings tensions for the country's interests and national security. Some of the other consider the ideological nature of the Islamic Revolution is the reason of the closeness and strengthening of relations with their Arab and Islamic neighbors so it is an opportunity for Iran's foreign policy. Saudi Arabia, which poses itself as the regional power, defines the developments in the Middle East as an area of regional rivalry with Iran.

The book examines Iran's foreign policy in the Middle East regarding the two countries: Saudi Arabia and Syria. The confrontation between the two regional powers (Iran and Saudi Arabia) will stay one of the most important and the debates will continue over the coming years. It also should be mentioned that the geopolitical role of Syria in the upcoming developments in the Middle East will only increase.

The object of this book is the foreign policy of Iran.

The subject is the main characteristics of the Iran's foreign policy regarding its relations with Saudi Arabia and Syria from the year of 2009.

The main goal. This book seeks to study the foreign policy approaches of the Islamic Republic of Iran in the Middle East region after the 1979 Iranian Revolution in two periods: during the leadership of Imam Khomeini and Imam Khamenei. By studying Syria and Saudi Arabia between 2009 and 2017, the author is examining the Iran's foreign policy in relation to the two countries. Therefore, **the following tasks** should be solved:

1. To determine the structure of Iran's decision-making process and underline the special features of it;

2. To estimate Iran's position and role in the Middle East, analyze the factors which promote the growing of it;

3. To establish the main characteristics of Iran's foreign policy and place that Saudi Arabia and Syria occupy in it;

4. To trace the dynamic of Iran-Syria relations throughout the post-revolutionary period starting with the Iran-Iraq war and after;

5. To examine Iran-Syria and Iran-Saudi Arabia relations before and after the Arab spring.

The degree of scientific elaboration of the topic. The foreign policy of Iran is well explained through multiple researchers but still author of the book finds that there is not enough literature on the foreign-policy making process since the Islamic Republic of Iran represents a unique government with the Islamic-oriented government.

Thus, the book of Iranian author Firoozabadi examines the main goals of the Iranian foreign policy.[1] The present book states that ideology, conceptual and normative structures are practically one of the most important determinants of Iranian foreign policy. It uses realism theory to explain the foreign policy of the Islamic Republic of Iran. Another author is Keyhan B.[2] The book "Foreign Policy of the Islamic Republic of Iran in the Middle East" was published by the Ministry of Foreign Affairs of the Islamic Republic of Iran in 2015 and examines the events of September 9, 2001 and Arabic developments in 2011. The book, in three chapters, sets out the goals and principles of foreign policy of the Islamic Republic of Iran in the region. It also examines Iran's practical policies toward the countries and ultimately the Iran-U.S. interaction. The September 11 terrorist events in the United States, followed by the massive presence of U.S. military forces in the region in the context of the two wars of Afghanistan and Iraq, brought direct political and security threats to Iran and subsequently seriously affected the orientation of Iran's foreign policy in the region. At that time, the main goal of Iran's foreign policy was to increase relative security through the containment

[1] 1.Dehghani Firoozabadi, Seyed Jalal, Discourse Transformation in the Foreign Policy of the Islamic Republic of Iran, Tehran, Iran Institute, 2005
Firoozabadi D., Jalal S. Discourse Transformation in the Foreign Policy of the Islamic Republic of Iran // Tehran, Iran Institute, 2005.
[2] Keyhan B. The foreign policy of Iran in the Middle East // The publishing house of the Ministry of Foreign Affairs, 2015.

of the American threat, and these developments necessitated the increase of the regional role of Iran in preventing the threat in foreign policy. The author of the book seeks to discuss the conceptual and theoretical contradictions arising from the presence or absence of Iran in regional affairs and its effects on its relations with supranational influential players, especially the United States. Author have also used an article of Seyyed Ali Nejat on the new regional developments including the Syrian war and the new attitudes of Iran towards it[3]. In his other researches[4] he examines the position of Iran on the revolutions in Tunisia, Egypt, Libya, Yemen and the developments in Bahrain and Syria. He concludes that the foreign policy of the Islamic Republic of Iran has been influenced by ideological and realistic factors in connection with the new developments in the region.

Another article examines the approach of the Islamic Republic of Iran in Syria (in the framework of the theory of games). Mohammad Ali Shahriari, Ismail Shafiei, Nafise Vaez[5] state that Syria has geopolitical, geostrategic, and geo-economic significance; therefore, it is the point of opposing forces. This research, analyzes descriptive and analyzes the foreign policy of the Islamic Republic of Iran towards Syria, using the game theory. Among the other Iranian researchers, we should mention the following: Afrasiabi K. L.[6], Adib-Moghaddam A.[7], Asisian N.[8], Djalili M.R.[9], Esfahani A.S.[10] and others.

Among the other authors is Furtig Henner and his articles[11] of the role of Iran after the Arab uprisings. The author refers to the foreign policy of Iran against the Arab countries and their motives for leading the region. The author has also used a lot of translated information, as, for example, Esposito J.[12], Sadjadpour K., Ben B[13].

---

[3] Nejat S.A. The Syrian crisis and regional gaps, 2015.
[electronic source]. Available at: https://www.cmess.ir/Page/View/11/11
[4] [electronic source]. Available at: https://www.cmess.ir/Page/Person/3/3
[5] Research of the approach of Iran towards Syria (in frames of the theory of games)
[electronic source]. Available at: http://pir.iaush.ac.ir/article_34402_930b421930b585d6a91e1e73512f319d.pdf
[6] Afrasiabi K. L. After Khomeini: New Directions in Iran's Foreign Policy // Westview Press. Boulder CO. 1994.

[7] Adib-Moghaddam A. Iran and the world after Rouhani // University of London, 2017-2018. [electronic source]. Available at: http://www.ide.go.jp/library/Japanese/Publish/Periodicals/Me_review/pdf/201709_01.pdf
[8] Asisian N. Russia & Iran: Strategic Alliance or Marriage of Convenience // Small Wars Journal, 2013.
[9] Djalili M.R. Iran-Iraq: radioscopie dune guerre ambigue, (Iran-Iraq: radioscopy of an ambiguous war) // Politique Internationale, 1983.
[10] Esfahani A.S. Cultural Globalization and Foreign Policy Strategies of the Islamic Republic of Iran (Case Study; the Seventh and the Ninth Governments) // Published by Canadian Center of Science and Education, 2017.
[11] [electronic source]. Available at: http://www.dw.com/fa-ir

[12] Espasito J. The Iranian revolution and its global reflection, translation by Doctor Shanechi M.M. Article issuing the Iranian revolution: politics, objectives and instruments, Ramezani R.K. // Tehran: Center for the recognition of Islam and Iran, 2003.
[13] Sadjadpour K., Ben B. Iran in the Middle East: leveraging chaos // FRIDE, a European think tank for Global Action, 2015. [electronic source]. Available at: http://fride.org/descarga/PB202_Iran_in_the_Middle_East.pdf

It has to be mentioned that the material of analytic centers was widely used. Firstly, materials of Institute for political and International Studies[14], Research Institute of Strategic Studies[15], Islamic Parliament Research Center of The Islamic Republic of Iran[16], Iran Research Academy[17] based in Iran. The following institutions are also making part of the research: Canadian research center, RAND, University of Saint Andrews, Brooking institution, Royal United Services Institute for Defense and Security Studies, Netherland Institute of International relations "Clingendael" and many others.

The sources of the research. The author has represented few groups of references in English and Persian languages.

The first group contains legislative documents. It includes primarily Constitution of the Islamic Republic of Iran since the first chapter has an explication of the political structure in Iran; information about it is represented the Articles of the Constitution.[18]

The second group has documents of international organizations, such as UN[19], IAEA[20].

The third group are publicistic documents, which represent interviews and speeches of the political leaders. [21] [22] Due to the role of the leader in Iran, it has particular importance.

The fourth group is historical sources.

Chronological framework. Because the foreign policy of Iran and Saudi Arabia in the Middle East are studied in the book, and there is a need to understand the role of these two countries in the Middle Eastern changes and the formation of alliances, the author suggested the period since 2009 until nowadays. As for Syria, it is studied as the sphere of the geopolitical interests of Iran.

Theoretical and methodological base. The author used analytic method, deduction, historical approach, problem and chronological and comparative methods. Thus, deduction method

---

[14] Institute for political and international studies. [electronic source]. Available at: http://ipis.ir/

[15] Research Institute of Strategic Studies. [electronic source]. Available at:http://www.riss.ir/

[16] Islamic Parliament Research Center Of The Islamic Republic of Iran. [electronic source]. Available at: http://rc.majlis.ir/fa

[17] Iran Research Academy. [electronic source]. Available at:http://iranresearchacademy.com/

[18] Iran (Iran Republic of)'s Constitution of 1979 with Amendments trough 1989 // [electronic source]. Available at: https://www.constituteproject.org/constitution/Iran_1989.pdf?lang=en

[19] Chapter VIII. Considerations of questions under the council's responsibility for the maintenance of international peace and security [electronic source]. Available at: http://www.un.org/ar/sc/repertoire/85-88/85-88_08.pdf

[20] Joint Comprehensive Plan of Action implementation and verification and monitoring in the Islamic Republic of Iran in light of United Nations Security Council Resolution 2231 (2015) // IAEA [electronic source]. Available at: https://www.iaea.org/sites/default/files/gov-2015-72-derestricted.pdf

[21] Khomeini: "We Shall Confront the World with Our Ideology" // Radio Iran, 1980. [electronic source]. Available at http://www.merip.org/mer/mer88/khomeini-we-shall-confront-world-our-ideology

[22] Islamic Republic of Iran, Permanent Mission to the United Nations, Address by H.E. Doctor Mahmoud Ahmadinejad President of the Islamic Republic of Iran before the Sixty-Second Session of the United Nations General Assembly // United Nations, 2007 [electronic source]. Available at: http://www.un.org/webcast/ga/62/2007/pdfs/iran-eng.pdf

was used to study the religious component of the political structure. Historical and chronological approaches gave a possibility to underline the stages of the development of the relations between the countries. The comparative method helped to find the common and the differences during the Khomeini and Khamenei.

Academic novelty. In this research, the academic novelty is represented through the new perspective on the relationship between Iran and Saudi Arabia in terms of sectarianism, in which the two countries are confronting; a clear example of which can be found in Yemen, Bahrain, etc. The study of Iran's foreign policy in the Middle East region in two different periods of leadership (Imam Khomeini, Imam Khamenei) after the 1979 revolution can be also seen as novelty. To make the following research valuable, the author have visited Saudi Arabia and spoke with different representatives of the universities to understand their points of view. Unfortunately, due to an existing crisis in Syria, the author did not have a chance to visit a country of study, but still hopes that his research would be a comprehensive work representing the scientific importance. The author has used a lot of comprehensive material in different languages, including the researchers of the Iranian analytical centers, which represent a special value due to the importance of the information, that has not been translated ever before. Also, in this work there is a competitive analysis of Iran's foreign policy throughout the years after the revolution in 1979. This approach helps explain the modern foreign policy of Iran and make clear why, for example, Syrian crisis has attracted Iran's attention as well to find out the competitive character of Iran-Saudi Arabia relations. What is also new in this book is the two models presented in the Chapter 1 made exclusively by the author. They explain the decision-making process, election process and the flow of information in this country.

Theoretical importance of this research. consists in the systematization and analysis of large amounts of historical material, the development of Iran's foreign policy, which, of course, can be a significant contribution to the fundamental science of history.

The main provisions and conclusions, presented in the book can be expanded and concretized in further research work.

The credibility of the work and approbation of the research. The provisions of this research were approved during the scientific and practical conferences of students, postgraduates and young scientists, held at the Peoples' Friendship University Russia, as well as at various seminars and round tables.

The main points of the book are also presented in articles of the author published in scientific journals included in the list of Higher Attestation Commission, and in various materials and scientific works, including author's two books.

The topic of the following research as well as the work on it were discussed at a meeting of the Department of theory and history of international relations of the People's Friendship University of Russia, was approved and recommended for defense.

Relaying on the previously published materials on the same or similar topics and the use of the author different retrospective and representative resources, verifiable, independent, comprehensive information, methods, approved in Russian and foreign historical science, the validity of the author's conclusions can be proved.

The main points for the defense

1.   Iran's foreign policy in the Middle East region after the Islamic revolution in 1979, and in particularly in the sphere of its relations with Saudi Arabia during the various presidential periods, was not tense. During the early years of the Islamic Revolution under the leadership of Imam Khomeini, Iran pursued idealistic policies. During the time of Imam Khamenei, it can be stated that Hashemi Rafsanjani and Mohammad Khatami chose the détente foreign policy with the countries of the Middle East and Saudi Arabia. During the presidency of Mahmoud Ahmadinejad, Iran's foreign policy has shifted to tensions with some countries, especially Saudi Arabia.

2.   Due to the nuclear crisis, Iran's influence in the Middle East region has changed throughout the period from 2009 to 2017. It is the result of the starting of the nuclear development by Iranian government. Despite the imposed sanctions it has made Iran on of the members of the so-called nuclear club. of Therefore, the regional rival of Iran, the kingdom of Saudi Arabia, has insecurities.

3.   During the presidency of Hassan Rouhani, who continues to be the president of Iran (2017), Iran's foreign policy in the Middle East is expanding its sphere of influence in the Middle East by resolving its nuclear issue, but being in the same time in confrontation with Saudi Arabia sectarian wars.

4.   As for Syria, it can be said that Iran's foreign policy is always considered to be a realistic one towards this country, and Iran's support for it is trying to maximize its sphere of influence and to support Hezbollah and the axis of resistance.

The structure of work. The book contains introduction, three chapters, conclusion and sources of the research.

Chapter 1. The basis and structure of Iran's foreign policy in the Middle East

1.1. Political and legal structure of Iran's foreign policy

The structure of power in the political system of the Islamic Republic of Iran is the same as in most of the countries, but due to the ideological nature of power, it has special features and complexity, which should be noted. On the one hand, the government in Iran is common with the other countries. The government structure in Iran has three branches: legislative, executive and judicial[23]. On the other hand, the political process in Iran has its own structure and hierarchy. In the legislature of the parliamentary elections in Iran two hundred nighty parliamentary seats are elected by the people for the period of four years. The president is elected by the people for four years; presidential term is two terms maximum for one person. The president, who is the executive head of the government, has the responsibility of managing all the current affairs of the country. The president proposes ministers to the Islamic Consultative Assembly. They are directly accountable to the parliament. But what distinguishes the Iranian system is the religious nature of it. Eighty-Six Islamic scholars are elected by the people as members of the Assembly of Experts for the period of eight years. Before that these scholars must already be approved by the Guardian Council. Then this institution chooses the Islamic Revolution Leader and monitors over his activity throughout his course. The head of the revolution appointed the head of the judiciary, which supervises all public, revolutionary and military courts. He is also the head of the armed forces. The Guardian Council of the Constitution is an institution responsible for complying with parliamentary approvals under Islamic law. It also provides interpretation of the constitution, and it is responsible for monitoring the good conduct of the presidential elections, parliament and Council of Experts. The Expediency Discernment Council of the System was established following some changes in the constitution in 1988. All thirty-eight members of this council are appointed by the leader among different political thoughts, parties and different populations. The responsibilities of the Expediency Council are to find ways to resolve the stalemate between the Parliament and the Guardian Council, if necessary, advising the leadership and proposing general strategies of policy of the Islamic Republic. Supreme National Security Council was established after a revision of the constitution. The president has headed the Supreme Council, and this council is a combination of the strategic institutions of the

---

[23] Article 160. Iran (Iran Republic of)'s Constitution of 1979 with Amendments through 1989 // [electronic source]. Available at: https://www.constituteproject.org/constitution/Iran_1989.pdf?lang=en (reference date: 01.05.2016).

Islamic Republic of Iran. The two representatives from the leadership, the heads of the three powers (the president, the speaker of the parliament and the head of the judiciary), the ministers of foreign affairs, the minister of internal affairs (of the interior), information, defense, the commanders of the armed forces, such as the army and the Islamic Revolutionary Guard Corps, are members of this council. The Supreme Council develops national security, foreign policy, defense policy and security policies of the system. Council resolutions are valid after the approval of the leadership. The modal (1) represents the main pillars of the Islamic Republic of Iran system (annexed to this chapter).

The constitution of the Islamic Republic of Iran clearly clarifies the priorities of Iran's foreign policy, which are: Muslims, neighbor countries and non-alignment movement[24].

But in fact, the four groups of countries are prioritized, respectively:

1.   Neighboring countries of Iran;

2.   Muslim countries;

3.   Third World Countries;

4.   Countries that represent political, economic, social or military needs of Iran.

Iran is situated between the important energy regions in the world: the Persian Gulf and the Caspian Sea. In the post-Cold War era, Iran emerged as a regional power in the southwestern Asia, and as his geostrategic importance raised, its influence in two larger regions: the Middle East, Central Asia and the Caucasus also increased. In each region, Iran's policies reflected Iran's economic and security needs. And for the same reason sometimes it happens that Iran's bilateral relations have multilateral character with countries of the same region. In the South, relations with the Gulf Cooperation Council (GCC) countries show a new attitude of Iran's foreign policy. In the Central Asia, Iran is generally willing to develop relations through multilateral policies. Especially, this may encourage the countries of this region to join the Organization of Economic Cooperation (ECO). In this context, it can also be mentioned that Iran's motive for cooperation with the Central Asia and Caucasus countries is economy.[25]

In the south, the main reason for Iranian cooperation in the Persian Gulf is the security due to the presence of the U.S. troops in the region.

The foreign policy of Iran and national power

Place of Iran in relation to the above-mentioned factors are the indicators of the country's strength and special position.

---

[24] Ardebili H. K. Return to Neither West nor East policy // Diplomatic Citizen, 1996.
[25] Afrasiabi K. L. After Khomeini: New Directions in Iran's Foreign Policy // Westview Press. Boulder CO. 1994.

Ideology. Islam represents a full pattern of thoughts, comprehensive belief that governs the thought, function of the system of the Islamic Republic and forms the values of it. The legitimacy of the system originates from the religion of Hanif[26], and the authority of the state, which is the source of the relation of power and value system, which comes from Islam. The development and expansion of real people's participation, the strengthening of the national spirit, and the unity among the Iranian people despite the cultural, racial and ethnic differences is one universal school of thought in the government. From this perspective, the goal of a foreign policy is based on ideology, affecting the environment, changing it according to its own needs. The foreign policy of the Islamic Republic of Iran, despite its short existence and experience, has achieved great goals through the principles of revolution in quite a large area of the world.[27]

Geographical factors. Iran is unique in terms of its size, shape, borders, and climatic status. It has fifteen neighboring countries with land and maritime borders between the four regions: Eastern Mediterranean, Persian Gulf, Central and Caucasian regions, and the Indian subcontinent.

Human-social factors. Among these factors is the population size, with seventy million people with a growth rate corresponding to the largest countries in West Asia and the Middle East.

Another factor is the national characteristics of the people. The spirit of the Iranian people in anti-hostility and safeguarding the national interests was the reason why Iran stood out from the war with Iraq.

Political factors. Government structure, decision-making and policy making in the country are such that they can be considered as sources of power. The role of leadership in the management of diplomacy and the presentation of economic, cultural, military and social goals of the countries are not covered. The Government of the Islamic Republic of Iran has a relatively efficient structure for orienting and implementing a coherent foreign policy. The existence of centers and institutions such as the leadership, the presidency, the Supreme National Security Council, the Islamic Consultative Assembly and the Ministry of Foreign Affairs made it possible for the country to consider its foreign policy in accordance with the mission of the Islamic Revolution, its principles and objectives, in a way that it is in the best of country's abilities. The international credibility of the country responds the current world standards of industrial development, scientific progress, high standards of living, etc.

---

[26] Religion of Hanif: Ḥanīf (Arabic, Ḥanīf; plural, ḥunafā') meaning "revert" refers to one who, according to Islamic belief, maintained the pure monotheism of the patriarch Abraham.
[2] Velayati A. A. First Speech // Foreign Policy Magazine No. 1. 1986.

Economic factors. Economic potential (capabilities) of each county is considered as one of the major criteria of national power. Economic indicators such as gross national product, income, quantity and quality of industrial and agricultural production, and access to resources show that all the factors are needed to build an advanced version of Iran.

Military Factors. What gives real importance to the geographic, natural resources and industrial capabilities is the military capability. The national strength of each country depends on the state, strength and preparedness of the armed forces. The Islamic Republic of Iran has been organized to have strong armed forces and popular support in the form of the Basij organization[28], so that the land can be protected from enemy's territorial title.[29]

Also, Iran has high position in military sector, having strong and large law enforcement force (Disciplinary Force of the Islamic Republic of Iran), possessing facilities, advanced military technology and industry, as well as a sufficient experience.[30]

Foreign Policy goals of the Islamic Republic of Iran

The most important source for understanding the goals of Iranian foreign policy is the Constitution of the Islamic Republic of Iran. In accordance with it the goals of Iran's cultural, social, political and economic system may be identified.

The totality of Iran's foreign policy goals by reviewing the Constitution may be seen as the following:

- Human happiness throughout human society as its ideal;[31]

- The negation of all kinds of oppression, authoritarianism, or the acceptance of domination, which secures justice, political and economic, social, and cultural independence and national unity;[32]

- The rejection of any kind of domination, both its exercise and submission to it; the preservation of the all-inclusive independence of the country and its territorial integrity; the defense of the rights of all Muslims; non-alignment in relation to the domineering powers; mutual peaceful relations with nonaggressive states;[33]

---

[28] The Basij (Persian: lit. "The Mobilization"), Niruyeh Moghavemat Basij (Persian: , "Mobilisation Resistance Force"), full name Sāzmān-e Basij-e Mostaz'afin (Persian: "The Organization for Mobilization of the Oppressed"),[4][5] is one of the five forces of the Islamic Revolutionary Guard Corps.

Maleki A. Foreign Policy of Iran // Italian Marco Polo Magazine. Naples, Institute of International Relations, Italy. 1997.

[30] Mohammadi M. Foreign Policy of the Islamic Republic of Iran. Principles and Issues of Tehran // Publishing House of Dastgostar. 1998.

[31] Article 154 Op. cit.
[32] Article 2 Op. cit.
[33] Article 152 Op. cit.

- The complete rejection of colonialism and the prevention of foreign influence[34], the complete strengthening of the national defense, through universal military training, with the aim of securing the country's independence, its territorial integrity, and its Islamic system[35];

- Preventing the economic dominance of foreigners in the national economy[36];

- In foreign domination over the natural and economic resources, foreign domination over culture, the army, and other affairs of the country, is forbidden;[37]

- Mutual peaceful relations with non-hostile states;

- Honesty and faith in the treaties.

In general, the objectives of foreign policy can be seen as following:

Foreign policy reflects the goals and policies of a government on the international relations scene and in relation to other states, communities and international organizations and global events.

National Goals. According to Articles 3, 9, 67, 121, 152, 153 of the Constitution national goals of the country include: incorporating Islam, liberty, universal independence, unity and territorial integrity, public participation, full strengthening of the national defense and enhancement.

Transnational goals are reflected in the following Articles of the Constitution: 3, 11, 152, 153, 154 and include the defense of the rights of Muslims, are the undeniable support of the oppressed of the world, the political, economic, and cultural unity of the Islamic world.

The structure of decision making in foreign policy of the Islamic Republic of Iran

In the Islamic Republic of Iran, there are political, social, religious, and economic groups that influence and react to the policies of the official organs. Among them are the houses of the Grand Ayatollahs, the Imams of Friday Prayer, the political parties, the Combatant Clergy Association, the Association of Combatant Clerics,[38] the Society of Seminary Teachers of Qom[39], the Revolutionary Institutions and the mass media. But foreign policy decisions have a hierarchy and a certain system. According to the Article 57 of the Constitution the system of governing is based on the separation of powers in the Islamic Republic of Iran which consist of the legislative, the executive, and the judiciary powers. Compilation of foreign policy and its implementation in Iran is mainly in the field of Leadership, Legislative and Executive Powers, where each one has

---

[34] Articles 3, 4, 5 Op. cit.

[35] Article 3-11 Op. cit.

[36] Article 43-8 Op. cit.

[37] Article 153 Op. cit.

[38] The Combatant Clergy Association (Persian translit: Jāme'e-ye Rowhāniyyat-e Mobārez) is a politically active group in Iran, but not a political party in the traditional sense.

[39] The Society of Seminary Teachers of Qom (Persian edition) was founded in 1961 by the leading Muslim clerics of Qom. It was founded by the students of Ayatollah Khomeini after his exile to Iraq in order to organize political activities of Khomeini's followers and promote his revolutionary interpretation of Islam such as the idea of Islamic government.

limited authority in this regard. The model (2) shows the relationships of these institutions with each other.

Leadership. Directly or indirectly an important part of foreign policy decisions is in the responsibility of the leadership. In accordance with the Article 110[40] of the Constitution, the authorities and responsibilities of the leader include declaring war, peace and mobilizing forces. On the other hand, all the decisions of the Supreme National Security Council (in relation to foreign policy), must be approved by the leadership and the leader has the authority to appoint two people in the council.

Presidency. According to the Article 113 of the Constitution after the leadership, the President of the Republic is the highest official of the country. He is responsible for executing the constitution and heading the executive power, except in instances that are directly related to the leadership. In the decision-making structure of foreign policy, the president, nominates and appointments of the minister of foreign affairs, ambassadors and representatives of the Islamic Republic of Iran, accepts foreign ambassadors residing in Tehran, signs protocols, agreements and treaties of the Government of Iran with other states, as well as signs treaties concerning the international unions, etc.[41]

The Cabinet of Ministers. The general policy governing the Islamic Republic of Iran is ensured through approvals and instructions from the leadership through the Cabinet of Ministers, considering the responsibilities of each of the ministries. At the beginning of each year, the government provides its annual program to the parliament, and the parliament adopts the program and allocates funds. It also plays an important role in the implementation of foreign policy. The establishment or termination of diplomatic relations, as well as the reduction and expansion of relations with other countries are under the supervision of an executive brunch. The Islamic Consultative Assembly[42] is the supreme institution of the country's legislature; in general, it can legislate within the limits of the Constitution of the country. The Islamic Consultative Assembly interferes through the adoption of all international treaties, conventions and international agreements in foreign policy. Also, any minor changes such as changes in border lines, referral to arbitration, obtaining or lending, as well as recruiting foreign experts is also in the responsibility of the Islamic Consultative Assembly.

---

[40] Article 110. Op.cit.

[41] Article 113. Op.cit.

[42] The Islamic Consultative Assembly (Persian: Majles-e Showrā-ye Eslāmī), also called the Iranian Parliament, the Iranian Majlis (or Majles,), is the national legislative body of Iran.

The Supreme National Security Council. Article 176 of the Constitution says that to protect national welfare, safeguard the Islamic Republic, and territorial integrity and national sovereignty, the Supreme Council of National Security is established under the leadership of the President of the Republic. Its duties are as follows:

- determining the defense and security policies of the country within the boundaries defined by the leadership;

- coordinating political, social, informational, cultural, and economical activities in relation to general defense and security concerns;

- benefiting from the country's material and spiritual resources in confronting domestic and foreign threats[43].

A major part of the work of the Supreme National Security Council[44] is within the scope of the country's foreign relations.

The Guardian Council of the Constitution[45]. According to the Articles 94 and 96[46] all legislation of the Islamic Consultative Assembly must be sent to the Guardian Council, which must evaluate it within ten days to assure its compatibility with the constitution and the Islamic criteria. The Council must return the legislation to the Assembly for reconsideration if it is incompatible; otherwise, the legislation can be executed. Many of the jurisprudents in the Guardian Council shall determine the compatibility of the proceedings of the Islamic Consultative Assembly with the commands of Islam. A majority of all the members of the Guardian Council shall determine the compatibility of the proceedings with the constitution. It should also be mentioned about the Expediency Discernment Council[47]. Though the Council has been recognized as the leading advisory arm, it can also resolve disagreements between the parliament and the Guardian Council. The Supreme Leader also delegates some of his authority to the Council.[48].

---

[43] Article 176. Op.cit.

[44] Supreme National Security Council (SNSC; Persian: Showrāye Āliye Amniyate Mellī) is the national security council of the Islamic Republic of Iran.

[45] The Guardian Council of the Constitution (Persian: , Shūra-ye negahbān-e qānūn-e āsāsī) is an appointed and constitutionally mandated 12-member council that wields considerable power and influence in the Islamic Republic of Iran.

[46] Articles 94, 96 Op. cit.

[47] The Expediency Discernment Council of the System (Persian Majma' Taškhīs Maşlaḥat Nezām) is an administrative assembly appointed by the Supreme Leader

[48] What are statuses and duties of the "Expediency Council" in the Iranian system? 2017.
[electronic source]. Available at:
http://english.khamenei.ir/news/5072/What-are-statuses-and-duties-of-the-Expediency-Council-in-the (reference date: August 21, 2017).

Judicial system of Iran. Although the judiciary is not directly involved in the decision-making process in Iran's foreign policy, the presence of this force exists in two parts. First, the cases related to the country's judicial developments and the obligation of the Ministry of Foreign Affairs to respond to human rights institutions such as, for example, the United Nations Commission on Human Rights and the Geneva Human Rights Committee. The second is overseeing the Ministry's activities by having the Administrative Court of Justice and the General Inspection Organization of Iran[49].

The Ministry of Foreign Affairs. In accordance with the Constitution and the Act on the Duties of the Ministry of Foreign Affairs, adopted on April 9, 1985, the Ministry of Foreign Affairs is responsible for the implementation of foreign policy, but the ministry's role is higher due to two reasons. First reason is that it is a member of most of decision-making structures, such as the Supreme National Security Council and the government. In other institutions such as the Islamic Consultative Assembly or the Expediency Council, the issue is discussed with the presence of a representative from the Ministry of Foreign Affairs. The second is that sometimes the issue needs to be solved quickly and for that the Ministry would not wait for a long time until the bureaucratic procedures are done. In these cases, the Foreign Minister decides and then reports to the other authorities. In addition, it has responsibility of the control, supervision, communication and provision of agents, as well as the gathering information for decision makers and policy makers. In this regard, the tasks of the Ministry of Foreign Affairs are the following:

• Permanent attention and caring about the international events and the internal situation of the countries as well as the preparation of the reports;

• Review, establishment, maintenance and development of the foreign relations of Iran with other governments and international organizations;

• Conducting negotiations and correspondence with foreign governments and international organizations;

• Office of Political Missions. Consulate of the Ministry of Foreign Affairs and monitoring of public authorities abroad;

• Carrying out and linking the various organs and the government with other governments.

Implementing of foreign policy

---

[49] Kar M. The future of Iran: judicial reform. Who are the judges in the Islamic Republic of Iran // Legatum Institute. [electronic source]. Available at:
https://www.li.com/docs/default-source/future-of-iran/2012-future-of-iran-by-mehrangiz-kar-who-are-the-judges-in-the-islamic-republic-of-iran.pdf?sfvrsn=2 (reference date: July 14, 2016).

Once the decision is made, policymakers must implement it. The implementation of foreign policy has a lot of difference with the implementation of domestic policies. In the domestic policy, the state guarantees the issuance of decisions by the sovereignty and control exercised over its own nationals. But in foreign policy, no state has control over the other government. The first stage in implementing foreign policy is a convincing explanation that the adopted policies are in the favor of a certain county.[50]

While bargaining (negotiation) continues, an actor who wants to implement a certain policy can use tools to involve others. The following should be mentioned about the foreign policy implementation tools and techniques:

- The political instruments mainly consist of efforts of skilled personnel. They can achieve a goal in a way that the political process will meet the interests of the country;

- The diplomatic instruments are composed of individuals who represent their government in certain countries. Their duty is negotiating with target countries to reach an agreement based on national interests.

- The information and communication tools are responsible for communicating with the public (shaping of public opinion) and the mass media of target countries;

- The economic instruments are mainly in the hands of rich and advanced countries and are one of the most common and most effective means of executing foreign policy. The more target country is dependent on the other, the more effective and decisive will be the policy.

- The military tool is usually used if there was an inadequacy and inefficiency of other tools.[51]

Process of decision-making in foreign policy of Iran

The foreign policy of the Islamic Republic of Iran is the result of complex and multilevel interaction between governmental and non-governmental actors. Each of these actors pursues different and sometimes even contradictory goals. But the decision-making process in Iran's foreign policy can be seen clearly enough[52].

In general, there are two perspectives on Iran's foreign policy, which has connections with Islamic or Iranian views. Islamic identity and Iranian identity, in the view of these two categories

---

[50]Moghattar H. Discussions on International Politics and Foreign Policy // Tehran, Faculty of Political and Social Sciences. 1979.

[51] Khoshghat M.H., Foreign Policy Decision-making Analysis // Tehran, Publishing institute, Ministry of Foreign Affairs. 1996.

[52] Lim K. National Security Decision-Making in Iran // Taylor & Francis. 2015. [electronic source]. Available at: http://www.tandfonline.com/doi/abs/10.1080/01495933.2015.1017347 (reference date: 13.05.2016).

governance is separated from one another. The first group sees the main identity of the Islamic Republic of Iran as coming from the Islamic Revolution with the aim of returning to Islamic values. People took to the streets because they had a feeling that Islamic culture was ignored by the Iranian government, the traditions of the Iranian society were forgotten, and injustice in international relations was intensified by the Iranian government, and especially the Shah and the United States[53].

For the Islamic Republic of Iran to survive, the following is proposed:

- Keeping Muslims in other countries as faithful allies;
- Establishing close relations with Islamic countries;
- Avoiding negotiating with the United States as the superpower responsible for humiliating the Islamic Ummah.

The second group believes that Iran is a nation-state, like any other political unity in the modern world, and should be a major player on the international scene. In this way, geopolitics and Iran's economic energy status also emphasizes its importance. The followers of this point of view consider international trade and establishment of political relations to be the most important means in the contemporary world for the preservation of the national interests of Iran. [54]

Shortly, it can be said that the Iranian political institutions were defined by the Constitution adopted after referendum in 1979 and revised, also after referendum, in 1989. They are based on two fundamental pillars, Islamic and Republican, which correspond to a double source of legitimacy of the power: the divine sovereignty (art. 2) and the popular will (Articles 1 and 6). The principle of velayat-e faqih forms the cornerstone of the institutional building. The army, law enforcement and justice are placed directly under his control. The Iranian system includes organizations and institutions resulting from the revolution that function as structures of duplication of the state apparatus and depend entirely on the Guide: the guardians of the revolution (pasdarans), a permanent body created to counterbalance the regular army, the Basijs, revolutionary tribunals and committees, and so on. Thus, the government structure clearly reflects the political regime and even its foreign policy orientation.

---

[53]Izadi B. Foreign Policy of the Islamic Republic of Iran // Tehran, Center. Qom Seminary Publishing, 1992.
[54] Maleki A. Op. cit.

Model (1)

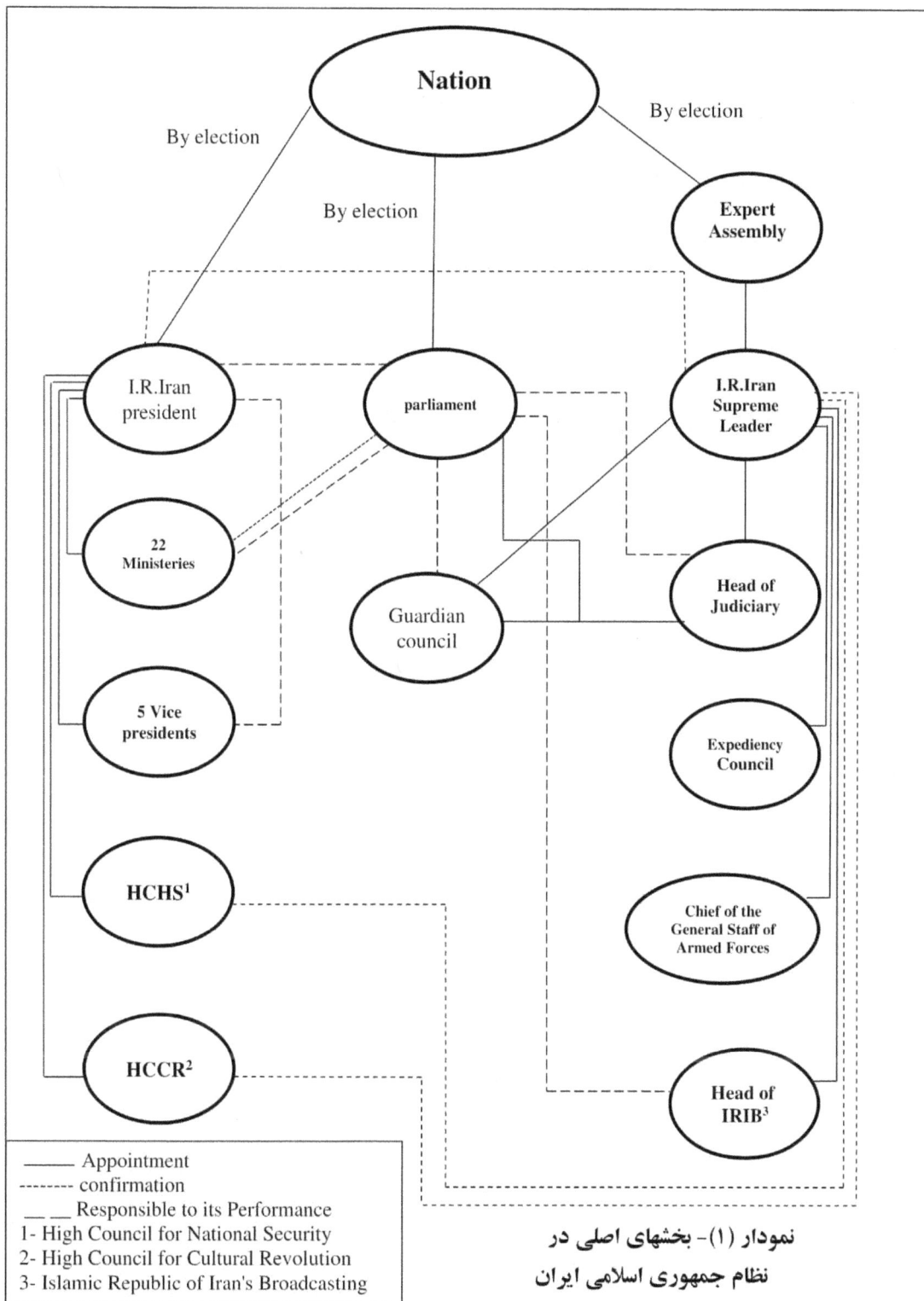

Nation

By election

By election

By election

Expert
Assembly

I.R.Iran
president

parliament

I.R.Iran
Supreme
Leader

22
Ministeries

Guardian
council

Head of
Judiciary

5 Vice
presidents

Expediency
Council

HCHS[1]

Chief of the
General Staff of
Armed Forces

HCCR[2]

Head of
IRIB[3]

——— Appointment
--------- confirmation
__ __ Responsible to its Performance
1- High Council for National Security
2- High Council for Cultural Revolution
3- Islamic Republic of Iran's Broadcasting

نمودار (۱)- بخشهای اصلی در
نظام جمهوری اسلامی ایران

21

Model (2)

`

An Opportunity Or Threat Outsides of Iran for Iran's National Interests

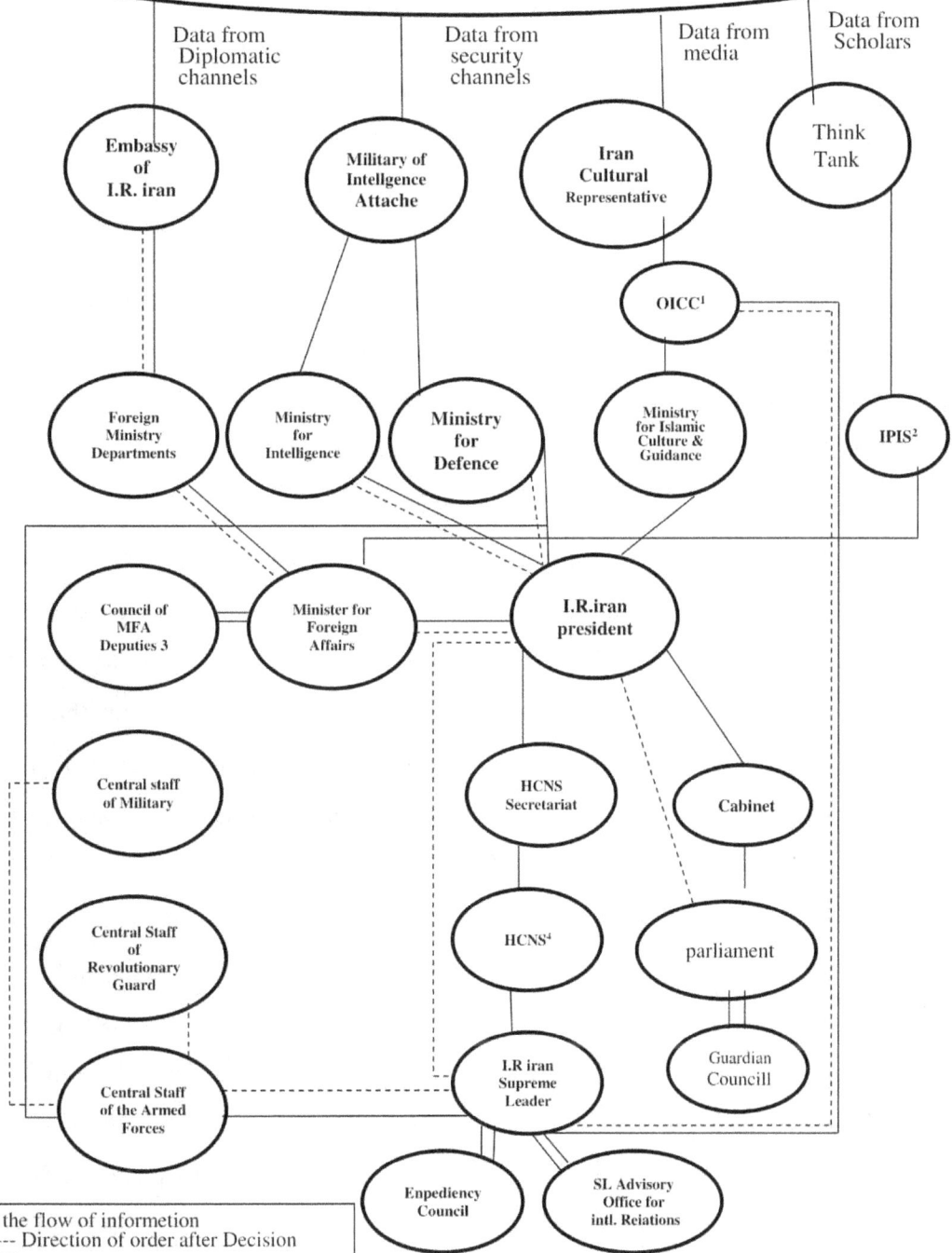

Data from Diplomatic channels

Data from security channels

Data from media

Data from Scholars

Embassy of I.R. iran

Military of Intelligence Attache

Iran Cultural Representative

Think Tank

OICC[1]

Foreign Ministry Departments

Ministry for Intelligence

Ministry for Defence

Ministry for Islamic Culture & Guidance

IPIS[2]

Council of MFA Deputies 3

Minister for Foreign Affairs

I.R.iran president

Central staff of Military

HCNS Secretariat

Cabinet

Central Staff of Revolutionary Guard

HCNS[4]

parliament

Central Staff of the Armed Forces

I.R iran Supreme Leader

Guardian Councill

Enpediency Council

SL Advisory Office for intl. Reiations

____ the flow of informetion
-------- Direction of order after Decision making
1- OICC: Organisation of Islamic culture and communication
2- IPIS:Institute for political and International studies
3- MFA: Ministry of Foreign Affalrs
4- HCNS: High Council for National Security

نمودار(۲)- ساختار تصمیم گیری در حوزه سیاست
خارجی در ایران

1.2. Economic, security, cultural and military basis of Iran in the Middle East

With the understanding of Iran's foreign policy, its status in the Constitution and the decision-making process of leaders, the goals of Iran in the region, especially its relations with neighboring countries and Muslim countries can be determined. Let us take a closer look at the position of this country in the Middle East in the economic, cultural and military dimensions. To understand Iran's economic, cultural, military, and security basics in the region, the Middle East status should first be identified. Then the position of the mentioned components in the regional policy of Iran is revealed. After that the geo-politic, geo-strategic, geo-economic and geo-culture of Iran is determined.

The Middle East represents a region that covers the Mediterranean Sea and the Persian Gulf and is geographically located at the intersection of continents of Europe, Asia and Africa, from Turkey to Europe and from the land of Egypt to the African continent. In this region there are various cultural and racial groups such as Iranian, Arabic, Barbarian, Turkish, Kurdish, Israeli, Assyrian, etc. The main languages of this region are Persian, Arabic, Turkish, Kurdish, Hebrew and Assyrian. The term "Middle East" was used for the first time in 1902 (1281 by the solar calendar) by an American historian Alfred Thayer Mahan to describe the region between the Far East and the Near East[55]. He suggested this in the article about the difficulties of the Persian Gulf for Britain in

---

[55] Karl E. Meyer. Editorial Notebook; How the Middle East Was Invented // The New York Times. 1991. [electronic source]. Available at:
http://www.nytimes.com/1991/03/13/opinion/editorial-notebook-how-the-middle-east-was-invented.html   (reference

the magazine "National Review" (NR). Shortly thereafter, this term was used by The Times national newspaper and then by the official correspondence of the British Government, and later by the governments of England and America in World War I and II. The term "Middle East" has been used since 1900, but it has also been possible that the term was used since the mid-nineteenth century in the Office of the Indian Affairs of the British Ministry of Foreign Affairs.[56]

Geographic area

Although today the Middle East is considered to be a wider region than Mahan intends, the importance and geostrategic significance of this term remain. For the same reason that there is difference between using terms "Middle East" and "Near East", the geographic area of this region and countries belong to it after the collapse of the Ottoman Empire is not clear. There is solidarity on the fact that some countries, as, for example, countries of the Persian Gulf region, the Fertile Crescent[57] plus Yemen, Turkey are in the Middle East. As for the countries of North Africa, Afghanistan, Pakistan and Cyprus by some of the researchers, are also considered to be a part of it. That is why the meaning of the Middle East has always been variable. Some have used it for the vast geographic description from the Indian subcontinent to North Africa, or to describe the Arab-Israeli conflict, while others consider the Persian Gulf and the Arabian Peninsula parts of it[58].

In the last decade, with the introduction of the Greater Middle East, a new definition has been added to the old ones. The boundaries of the Middle East have many times changed in the political, regional and international literature. The term "New Middle East" has been taken from the title of the book given by former Israeli Foreign Minister Shimon Peres after the assassination of Yitzhak Rabin in 1993. The book outlines the principles and objectives of the New Middle East Peace Initiative[59][60]. In this plan, issues should only be pursued through political negotiations, but after a decade it became clear that, firstly, needs from outside the region and presented by dominant powers cannot be implemented in all areas, and secondly the removal of nations to create a new order is not acceptable. Therefore, after the failure of the New Middle East plan, the United States

---

date: 10.06.2016).

[56] Lasdayr D., Blake J. H. The geopolitics of the Middle East and North Africa, translated by Mirheydar D., (Mohajerani) // Tehran. The office of political and international studies. 1992.

[57] The Fertile Crescent (in Persian: also known as the cradle of civilization) is a crescent-shaped region containing the comparatively moist and fertile areas of what is an otherwise arid and semi-arid Western Asia, the Nile Valley and Nile Delta.

[58] Shokooee, H. The term and concept of the Middle East: the Failure of a Geographical Term, Tabriz // University Journal of the Faculty of Literature and Humanities. 1968.

[59] Peres S., Naor A. The New Middle East // Henry Holt & Co; 1 edition. 1993.

[60] Also The term "New Middle East" was introduced to the world in June 2006 in Tel Aviv by U.S. Secretary of State Condoleezza Rice in replacement of the older and more imposing term, the "Greater Middle East."

came up with another plan of the Greater Middle East to create order, and change the look from the bottom, focusing on the lower levels of the societies in the region.[61]

The term "Greater Middle East", as well as the term "Middle East", was introduced by the West, for the first time developed by the American neoconservatives and entered the terminology of political science[62]. This term is the result of Western idea in the division of the world in terms of geopolitical importance. Although document of the "Greater Middle East" plan doesn't clearly state which countries make a part of it, it seems that from the point of view of initiators, the Greater Middle East stretch and expand from the Maghreb in North Africa and the Horn of Africa to the direction of the Arab countries, Turkey, Iran, Afghanistan, and the former Soviet republics in the Caucasus and Central Asia, covering Pakistan, Bangladesh and other territories to the Chinese borders. In this way, the Greater Middle East includes several countries that have very different political, social, cultural and economic structures, but American theorists use the term to seek a common point among all the mentioned countries.

The choice of the name for the term "Greater Middle East" by the American theorists was made to cover all countries that have an impact on the changes in the Islamic world. Therefore, in determining the limits of the Greater Middle East, the U.S. strategic thinkers with possible Israeli consultation, gave a name to this space from the countries of North Africa, such as Morocco and Algeria to the countries of Central Asia, such as Uzbekistan and Tajikistan, and other countries of the region, such as Afghanistan and Pakistan, and even Bangladesh and Indonesia. From the point of view of these theorists, the subject that represents the biggest threat in this region for the security and survival of Israel and consolidation of the U.S. hegemony in XXI century is not weapons of mass destruction, but the new behavior of the Muslims caused by the fundamental transformation of culture and political beliefs. Since the Middle East term is a regional cultural identifier, there is a controversy about the geographic area and composition of the country and the number of countries; some geographers include countries of North and East Africa while others count countries like Pakistan and Afghanistan as the Middle East.[63] Therefore, there is no exact definition of this region

[61]Syefulla S. Negah-I be tarh-e khavar-e miyane-ye bozogr. (Seyfulla S. A look at the Greater Middle East). [electronic source]. Available at: http://www.aftabir.com/articles/view/politics/world/c1c1223882561_the_middle_east (reference date: 05.05.2016).

[62] Nazemroaya M.D. Plans for Redrawing the Middle East: The Project for a "New Middle East" //GlobalResearch. 2016.
[electronic source]. Available at:
https://www.globalresearch.ca/plans-for-redrawing-the-middle-east-the-project-for-a-new-middle-east/3882 (reference date: 01.01.2016).

[63] Herzig, E. Islam, Transnationalism and Sub-regionalism in Cis countries, translated by Ejtehadi, A. // Quarterly Journal of Central Asia and the Caucasus, 2000.

in the composition of countries, but in general, the countries of this region are: Jordan, the United Arab Emirates, Iran, Bahrain, Turkey, Syria, Iraq, Saudi Arabia, Oman, Qatar, Kuwait, Lebanon, Egypt, Yemen and both Israel and Palestine, which include area of the West Bank and the Gaza Strip. The western countries of the region (Algeria, Tunisia, Libya and Morocco) are considered to be part of the Middle East because of their stronger historical and cultural dependency. Sudan is one of those countries. African countries, such as Mauritania and Somalia also have links with the Middle East. Turkey and Cyprus, which, from the perspective of geography are situated in and near this region, partly consider themselves as Europe (also this point of view is not supported by the whole society, thus it is contradictory). Iran is considered to be the eastern border of the Middle East, but sometimes it is considered to be Afghanistan (as part of this division). In this way, more than one fifth of the world's population lives in the territory of the Middle East.

Security and strategic position of the Middle East
Historical, cultural and religious importance

The Middle East has been one of the first origins in the world's civilization. Many of the world's beliefs have come from here. The Middle East is the birthplace of important religions such as Judaism, Christianity and Islam, and the holy places of these three religions are also located in this area. The first human find has been here. The world's first laws are written here, etc.

The perspective of geo-culture

The Middle East, from the cultural and historical and perspective is the origin and birthplace of the great religions of monotheism and divine. More than half of the nearly twenty known civilizations have been identified in the Middle East. Many other famous civilizations, such as the Chinese and Indian civilizations have also been recognized nearby the Middle East. From the perspective of religion, the city of Jerusalem is very sacred and valuable for the followers of the divine religions of Judaism, Christianity and Islam. In addition, the Middle East is the cradle of legislation and the knowledge of philosophy and literature, and so on. The art of the old world originated in this region and has spread all over the world.[64]

Economic importance

Although the Middle East and its heart, the Persian Gulf region, have an ancient civilization, history and culture, but what makes this region so important in the world is the energy mines,

---

[64] Etaat J. Geopolitical Characteristics of the Middle East // Series on Middle East Studies, 1996.

especially its oil, a concession that no other feature can compete with. This region has the largest energy reserves in the world. The well-known oil reserves of the Persian Gulf countries have 360 billion barrels, representing 64% of the world's oil reserves belonging to seven Gulf States[65]. The most important and largest oil reserves in Saudi Arabia have 163.2 billion barrels, Kuwait 65.4, Iraq 59, Iran 56, Emirates 5.7, Qatar 3.7, and Bahrain 2.4. In this way, oil revenues from these countries represent more than two thousand and five billion dollars from 1973 to 1993. According to the report of the Independent Petroleum Association of America (IPAA), the member countries of the OPEC, have 8.4 billion barrels, this is about 78% of the world's oil reserves, while only 6.5% of world crude oil consumption is related to these countries[66].

Among these countries, Saudi Arabia, Iraq, the UAE, Kuwait, Iran and Venezuela hold 70 percent of the world's reserves, and the five main Gulf oil producing countries (Saudi Arabia, Kuwait, Emirates, Iraq, Iran) have about 81 percent of the OPEC reserves, one of the most important oil producers and exporters of the crude oil which, regardless of them, cannot recognize OPEC and its structure, nor examine the global oil market and assess its future developments. In this comparison, the United States alone accounts for more than 25% of the world's oil production, while it has less than 3% of world crude oil reserves[67]. Europe has less than 12% of the world's oil reserves and accounts for more than 21% of world crude oil consumption, Japan with more than 7% crude oil have substantially less amount of oil reserves. Given the dependence and single product of the Middle East countries, especially in the Persian Gulf, to the oil industry, which accounts between 95% and 100% of the foreign exchange earnings of these countries, including Iran selling oil, it seems that two points have great importance: first, even with huge oil revenues in the Persian Gulf, including Iran and the Middle East, there is still a long way to become industrialized, and secondly, it can be easily understood that the security of this region and the flow of oil for the countries of the region as well as importers is crucial and vital. How did oil turn into a strategic commodity and gave the Persian Gulf a tremendous position in the third millennium so that no region in the world cannot be compared in terms of it.

---

[65] International Energy Outlook // Energy Information Administration Office of Integrated Analysis and Forecasting U.S. Department of Energy Washington, 2007.
http://test.ricerchetrasporti.it/wp-content/uploads/downloads/file_1235.pdf (reference date: 30.04.2016).
[66] Annual report // Organization of the Petroleum Exporting Countries, 2016. [electronic source]. Available at: http://www.opec.org/opec_web/static_files_project/media/downloads/publications/AR%202016.pdf (reference date: 01.10.2016).
[67] Clemente J. U.S. Oil Production Will Continue To Grow, 2016. [electronic source]. Available at: https://www.forbes.com/sites/judeclemente/2016/08/09/u-s-oil-production-will-continue-to-grow/#2235c0442677 (reference date: 17.05.2016).

In addition, according to forecasts, in the next 25 years, the world's oil reserves, except for the four major countries: Iran, Saudi Arabia, Iraq, and Kuwait, will come to an end so that the countries that currently have oil will need the oil from the Persian Gulf in future[68]. Of course, having oil reserves alone is not an opportunity, as the largest part of these opportunities has come from the West, especially the United States, in consuming and storing oil. In the countries of the Persian Gulf, in addition to producing oil, natural gas is one of the sources that, due to the abundance of its reserves, added the importance of this region in the Middle East. As the Persian Gulf countries have about 30% of the world's total gas reserves, Iran is in abundant supply of gas, and in terms of production and extraction it is at the head of the Persian Gulf. In the petrochemical industry the Middle East region plays a major role in the advancement of the economy and the development of the industrial nations of the world, and a quarter of the industrialized product of the developed countries of Europe is supplied by the petrochemical industry of the Middle East. Every year 330 thousand tons of urea, 100 thousand tons of sulfuric acid, 20 thousand tons of melanin, 5 thousand tons of ammonia and methanol per day are exported from the Persian Gulf countries to Europe, the United States and Oceania[69].

Strategic and military significance

The Middle East is the intersection of the three continents of Asia, Europe and Africa, and includes the territories and waterways that are among the most important geostrategic areas of the world. The strategic and military significance of the Middle East, in terms of its proximity to the two oceans: Atlantic and Indian, and the presence of the seas, such as the Mediterranean Sea, the Red Sea, the Caspian Sea, the Black Sea and the Persian Gulf, have long been regarded as the focal points of global power. In addition, strategic canals and straits such as the Suez Canal (the interface between the Mediterranean and the Red Sea in Egypt), the Strait of Hormuz (the Persian Gulf and Oman Sea), the Straits of Bosphorus and Dardanelles or the Turkish Straights (in the northwest of Turkey), the Strait of Bab-el-Mandeb (Red Sea to The Gulf of Aden in the southwest of Saudi Arabia), the Strait of Gibraltar (connecting the Mediterranean with the Atlantic) have multiplied the prominent role of the Middle East. Among the strategic areas of the Middle East, the Persian Gulf and Strait of Hormuz, in terms of strategy and geo-strategy is one of the fourteen major points of the

[68] Yusgiantoro P. Petroleum will still be the major energy resource in the 21st century, 2004. [electronic source]. Available at: http://www.opec.org/opec_web/en/902.htm (reference date: 18.02.2016).
[69] Aitani A.M.,, Halim S.H. Downstream in the Persian Gulf-2 //King Fahd University of Petroleum & Minerals. Oil and Gaz Journal. 1997. [electronic source]. Available at: https://www.researchgate.net/profile/Abdullah_Aitani/publication/258258689_DOWNSTREAM_IN_THE_PERSIAN_GULF-2_The_Persian_Gulf%27s_petrochemical_industry_is_proliferating/links/02e7e527a3a577a551000000.pdf?origin=publication_list (reference date: 18.02.2016).

world, and according to the Theory of Admiral (Alfred Mahan, 1902), the Persian Gulf is the Heartland of the earth and its domination means dominating the whole universe[70]. And this is what has been considered by the militarist powers from the distant past. With the end of the medieval period in Europe, the beginning of the Renaissance and the knowledge of Europeans from the wealth of the Middle East increased their motivation to dominate the Persian Gulf, and the Portuguese (in 1497), the Dutch (1607), the French (1680s), England in the XIX and XX centuries, and the Americans, since the end of the World war II, have struggled to control it all. Even though part of the Gulf oil exports to the European consumer countries through the pipeline, daily from the Strait of Hormuz from 15 to 20 million barrels of oil is transported by oil giant oil, while hundreds of commercial ships daily pass through this waterway.

Understanding the importance and position of the Middle East can now be studied in terms of its dimensions to Iran.

Geo-economical position of Iran

Iran is located in the southwest of Asia, owning a privileged geostrategic position to supply other countries with energy, and so has been a world-class focal point, which gave a special role to Iran's existing capacity to supply energy to different countries.[71] Because of its potential, such as the privileged geopolitical position, the abundant gas resources, and access to high seas and the strategic Strait of Hormuz, it has a monopoly position in supplying Asia of oil and gas comparing to other competing countries such as Turkmenistan, Qatar and Russia[72], using these variables Iran can turn into a superior regional power. Iran, on the other hand, has an important transit location, due to geopolitical advantages, on the international crossroads. These four routes connect Africa to Asia and Asia to Europe. In addition, Iran is linked to high seas and has a position that allows the access of Central Asian and Caucasian countries to the high seas and can play a role in swap or oil and gas transfers, fuel of Central Asian producers for countries such as Afghanistan and Pakistan.[73]

Geo-economic capabilities and advantages of Iran

Iran is recognized as the most important Persian Gulf country, and one of the main key actors of the regional energy events. Therefore, it can be argued that Iran, in addition to its geo-political credentials, has a unique value and capabilities in the field of geo-economics. One of these

---

[70] Singh P. Conceptual understanding of geopolitics with special reference to Indian Ocean // International Journal of Applied Research, 2015. [electronic source]. Available at: http://www.allresearchjournal.com/archives/2015/vol1issue6/PartF/1-5-109.1.pdf (reference date: 03.06.2016).

[71] Sheikhattar, A., 2006 The roots of political behavior in Central Asia and the Caucasus, p. 11,Tehran: Ministry of Foreign Affairs, third vol.

[72] Ibis.

[73] Sariolghalam M. Political Stability and Political Development: The Case of Iran // Political-Economic Quarterly, 1999.

capabilities is the location of Iran along the Persian Gulf, which is the world's fossil energy source in Hartland. In the north, there is the Caspian Sea, which is the second priority of the world's energy. Therefore, Iran's geopolitical and geo-economic link to the Caspian Sea and Central Asia with its position in the Persian Gulf, which controls more than half of the area, is a major factor in expanding Iran's resources and role in Asia and Europe. Any attempts of other countries to ignore this geo-political and geo-economic component of Iran, and exerting pressure on this country in the Persian Gulf and, lately in the Caspian Sea will lead to a negative reaction of other countries.[74] Other geo-economic capabilities of Iran can be cited by the growing need of developing countries in East Asia. Iran is the only country that due to its geo-political position and its abundant energy resources, can meet the needs of these countries. These countries are trying to escape the domination of American decision-making. Therefore, they want to have a close relationship with the only country that has independent policy from the United States in the region of the Caspian Sea and the Persian Gulf. China, possessing its double-digit economic growth, tried a lot to expand its energy partnerships with other countries and Iran is one of them. Iran is now a major center of gravity in China's energy security architecture.[75] Since China and Europe are calling for the polarization of the world in the XXI century, they consider themselves to be one of the poles of power in international relations; therefore, they are trying to achieve the elements of power, especially the elements of economic development, which means constant supply of energy. Since China and Europe will be the rivals of the U.S. in the XXI century, it is rational to seek solutions to ensure that they provide a constant supply of energy for themselves. Therefore, the special and unique position of Iran can be the best option for energy supplying for these countries.

The Persian Gulf has traditionally been the political-security center, as well as the focus of Iran's economic activities, but due to the victory of the revolution, efforts of the United States and the favorable opinion of the Persian Gulf states its influence has been diminished. In this way strategic orientation to the North, which is the Caspian Sea, Central Asia and the Caucasus allows Iran to compensate its luck of influence in the Persian Gulf region and prevent US policy of unilateralism in the region of Central Asia and the Caucasus, defeating its dominant strategy[76]. But despite these issues, the central role of Iran has been challenged due to its geo-economic status in the

---

[74]Khavar-e miyane va naqhsh-e geoghrafi-ye iran dar mantaghe (The Middle East and the geographical position of Iran in the region), 2010. [electronic source]. Available at: http://siasatrooz.ir/vdcgty9n.ak9tn4prra.html (reference date: 06.02.2016).

[75] Daniels O., Brown C. China's Energy Security Achilles Heel: Middle Eastern Oil // The Diplomat, 2015. [electronic source]. Available at: https://thediplomat.com/2015/09/chinas-energy-security-achilles-heel-middle-eastern-oil/ (reference date: 06.02.2016).

[76] Vaezi M. Geopolitics of crisis in Central Asia and Caucasus // Tehran: Institute for political and international studies Press, 2007.

development of regional partnership and transforming of the exceptional geo-economic position into political power, which could raise Iran's status on the international level. Firstly, there is a need for a good study of the country's economic capabilities, both potential and actual, investment in the region, which later should be considered in its foreign policy. One of the ways to transfer these resources to the high seas is Iran, which is the shortest, cheapest and safest way. On the other hand, the transmission of oil and gas pipelines will have a positive impact on Iran's national security. In addition, it should be noted that the special geopolitical situation of Iran is such that through the flow of oil and gas pipes from Iran's land lead to a wider expansion of its geo-economic cooperation with the republics of Central Asia and the Caucasus, where cooperation in the energy sector leads to economic cooperation, which ultimately leads to the geo-political integration of Iran with the Caspian Sea region. Also, the emphasis on energy, economic cooperation and broad political coordination can be a source of trust building in the region.[77]

The end of the Cold War and the collapse of the Soviet Union have created the new priorities in international instruments of influence, so that economic tools became more important. Also, there was a change and transformation in geo-political and geo-strategic regions and the division of new regions became more based on economic factors and geo-economical positions. In the meantime, the position and strategic role of the Middle East can be better understood, according to the words of Jordis von Lohausen, the retired general of the Austrian army, who believes that the Middle East is the center of the old world.[78] The center situated in the heart of the Persian Gulf region, known as the "center of the center". Thus, in the new millennium the geopolitics of the Persian Gulf went through a fundamental transformation. In the past geopolitical theories, the Persian Gulf was considered to be marginal land (periphery). In the new geopolitical theories, the Persian Gulf has become the axis of the heartland. While military strategies played a major role in the twentieth century, domination of strategic geographic territories became important, so that the one who controls resources and energy lines, especially oil and gas has the power of the world. The position of Iran is one of the most important among the countries of the Persian Gulf. While having a strategic position during the Cold War, in the new century, this factor has been adapted to the geo-economic perspective and its regional position has become international[79].

[77] Sheikh Attar A. The roots of political behavior in Central Asia and Caucasus // Tehran: Institute for political and international studies Press. 1994.

[78] Branckaert J. Musings of a Eurasian future // Journal of Eurasian Affairs, 2013. [electronic source]. Available at: http://www.eurasianaffairs.net/musings-of-a-eurasian-future/ (reference date: 06.02.2016).

[79] Pollack K. M. Containing Iran // The Iran Primer. United States Institute of Peace, 2010. [electronic source]. Available at: http://iranprimer.usip.org/sites/default/files/Containing%20Iran.pdf (reference date: 07.02.2016).

This exceptional and in the same time inevitable status can play a major role in drafting strategy of the systems of power of the century. In the Persian Gulf region and the Gulf of Oman, Iran has more than 2,000 km of coast appropriate for operating and many strategic islands; in the North it has border with the second largest source of oil and gas in the world. Even though Iran has about 17 percent of the world's gas reserves, it does not play a role according to its reserves in global markets. Exports of Russia through the pipeline in 2003 were 454.87 billion cubic meters of gas. Russia possesses 30% of the world's proven gas reserves, a share equivalent of 29% in total. Algeria possesses 9.2 % of proven gas reserves and a share of about 10% of the world's total gas exports. Qatar's share of the gas export market is 3.2%, while Iran's share in the gas export market is only 0.76%, it is in the 16th place among the countries exporting gas through the pipeline. In the case of liquefied gas, Iran's share is 0.5%[80].

On the other hand, the largest potential market for Iranian gas exports is the European Union market, which will reach 725 billion cubic meters of natural gas in 2025. The EU countries account for only 2% of the world's natural gas reserves, while their global gas consumption is more than 16%.[81] Even though in the spaces of new geo-economy Iran plays a vital role especially in the Middle East region in general and the Persian Gulf in particular, it can be the only country that, while dominating in the northern coast, has special capacities for acting in the Persian Gulf. However, Iran is deprived of the geopolitical leadership in the region and its impact on the production policies and energy transmission.

It should also be noted that Iran is capable of acting in multidimensional level. This actor can create economic-political connections and to preserve and strengthen them in this field. Iran, as one of the Middle East oil producers, transmitter and facilitator in the field of energy supply, also has another great point, and that is the domination on the backbone of the Middle East geo-economy, by connecting different geo-political regions. In other words, Iran is considered to be the first regional actor in the geo-strategic plans of the great powers.

Geo-cultural position of Iran

Considering the dimensions of Iran's civilization, especially in the field of Islamic and Iranian civilization, the Middle East is situated in two regions. The sacred Shi'a religious centers in

---

[80] Tarr D.G. Export Restraints on Russian Natural Gas and Raw Timber: What are the Economic Impacts? // CEPE Working Paper No. 74, 2010. [electronic source]. Available at: https://www.ethz.ch/content/dam/ethz/special-interest/mtec/cepe/cepe-dam/documents/research/cepe-wp/CEPE_WP74.pdf (reference date: 08.02.2016).

[81] Makinen H. The future of natural gas as the European Union's energy source – risks and possibilities // Electronic Publications of Pan-European Institute, 2010. [electronic source]. Available at: https://www.utu.fi/fi/yksikot/tse/yksikot/PEI/raportit-ja-tietopaketit/Documents/M%C3%A4kinen_final.pdf (reference date: 08.02.2016).

Karbala and Najaf in Iraq and the seminaries of the holy cities and clerics highlight the importance of these centers. Its religious leaders, such as Akhund Khorasani[82] and Naini[83] played a special role in the field of thought (intellectual field). Nowadays Iranian Ayatollah Sistani[84] plays an important role in the changes in Iraq.

Such religious centers in Syria, such as, for example, the ones of Zaynabiyah[85] witnessed Iranian pilgrimage before the civil war. The presence of Rass al-Hussein in Egypt and the Egyptian people in the Prophet's family shows the status of Iran in Egypt, while the two countries have a long history of civilization. The Shi'ites of Lebanon and Bahrain as well as the Zaidis of Yemen, and especially the Shiites in the Gulf States in Saudi Arabia and Kuwait, show this position better. In this way, the geo-cultural position of Iran is both religious and civilized in Bahrain and Iraq, and in some minorities in the region, such as Kurds. Iran, in relation to them, uses common cultural and civil elements (such as Nowruz, Persian language, mythological characters), common culture and history[86]. Finally, it should be noted that Iran is located at the regional center, which is the focus of the political space governing the energy economy; it emerges as a new regional power and plays a leading role in the diplomatic engagement of the Middle East. Therefore, its security is established in a situation where its main line is a harmony with a dominant space in the Middle East. The Middle East, as the centerpiece of global security and Iran at the heart of security in the Middle East are all connected, so that Iran plays key role in regional and world security. Due to its specific characteristics, including geo-politics, culture, history and economic fields, Iran is a productive actor in the Middle East. The constructive nature of Iran's role due to a possible instability and insecurity, lack of social, political and economic progress can endanger the national interests of Iran on the regional level. In other words, the national interests of Iran require that in any regional project, it will support the progress of the nations of the region. Due to these characteristics, the Islamic Republic of Iran can play a constructive role in implementing the great Middle East plan, including

---

[82] Mohammad Kazem Khorasani or Akhund-e Khorasani (1839-1911) was Twelver Shi'a Marja, politician, philosopher, reformer. He's regarded as one of the most important Shia Mujtahid at the time.

[83] Mohammad Hussein Naini Qaravi was Iranian Twelver Shia Marja', the most competent student of Ayatollah Kazem Khorasani.

[84] Al-Sayyid Ali al-Husseini al-Sistani or Sayyed Ali Hosseini Sistani , commonly known as Ayatollah Sistani in the Western world (born August 4, 1930), is a Shia marja in Iraq and the head of many of the seminaries (Hawzahs) in Najaf. He is described as the spiritual leader of Iraqi Shia Muslims and one of the most senior clerics in Shia Islam.

[85] Zaidiyyah or Zaidism (Arabic: az-zaydiyya, adjective form Zaidi or Zaydi) is one of the Shia sects closest in terms of theology to Sunni Islam. Zaidiyyah emerged in the eighth century out of Shi'a Islam. Zaidis are named after Zayd ibn 'Alī, the grandson of Husayn ibn 'Alī who they recognize as the fifth Imam.

[86] Barry J., Arbarzadeh S. State identity in Iranian foreign policy // British Journal of Middle Eastern Studies, 2016. [electronic source]. Available at: http://www.tandfonline.com/doi/abs/10.1080/13530194.2016.1159541?src=recsys&journalCode=cbjm20 (30.12.2016)

political development and democratization, economic progress, as well as social development and advancement. On the contrary, Iran's support for such plans, above all, requires the granting of a proper regional role to them and the status of Iran, on the one hand, which provides grounds for the use of Iran's intrinsic characteristics for regional peace and security. On the other hand, satisfying Iran's legitimate demands to maintain its security is the priority, while capacity building is on the second and regional levels.

1.3. Iran's foreign policy towards Syria and Saudi Arabia

Syria

In pre-Islamic times during the Achaemenid and Sassanian empires, Syria was the place of conflict and war between Iran, Greece and Rome, and was regarded as a kind of western border of the Great Iran. After the rise of Islam and until the World War I Syria was a part of territory of the Islamic empire. Syria is one of the countries where confrontation and action of three factors: geographic, power and politics have led to the formation of a kind of international competition for the influence and management of the internal events of the country. Syria is part of the Levant, which borders Lebanon, Cyprus, the occupied Palestine, Jordan, Iraq, and Turkey. For many years this country has had an ideological and political rivalry with the Iraqi Ba'ath government in the region; it has controversy over the Kurdish issue as well as disputes over the geographical factors with Turkey and has supported the Islamic Republic of Iran during the eight-year war against Iraq. It is also should be mentioned that Syria is located near the Occupied Palestinian Territory, which is the heart of the Middle East, and the center of multi-variable equation of the region[87].

Syria is one of the main geopolitical actors; it is linked to three factors in the strategic region of the Middle East. In the East it is located next to the important Mediterranean Sea and possesses 186 kilometers of coastline with the border countries of the region. Due to the same importance and strategic role, many international relations experts call "Syria the largest small country in the world".[88]

Position of Syria in relation to Iran

It can easily be said that in recent years, perhaps, none of the Arab states that have developed, do not have strategic and geopolitical significance as much as Syria does. To name the

---

[87]Niakuyi S., Bahmanesh H. Opposite actors in the Syrian crisis: goals and approaches // Foreign Relations Quarterly Journal, 2012.
[88]Rajabi S. Analysis of the Syria's Strategic Position in Regional and International Relations, 2012.

reasons why Iran supports Syria, it should be noted that Syria plays a vital role in Iran's strategic ties to the Mediterranean and the Near East and, as far as we can see Iran follows the developments/changes of the country regarding its interests. The relations between Tehran and Damascus have had a positive and growing trend since the independence of Syria in the early 1940s; there were common ideological aspects between the Shiites of Iran and the Syrian Alawis, existence of the pragmatism and common interests of the two governments. The policies of Israel and sovereignty of Ba'athist regime[89] of Saddam provided a solid ground (common enemy) to deepen relations between Iran and Syria. The four-day visit of Hafez al-Assad to Iran, lending 300 million to the Empire in Damascus, establishment of the Iranian embassy in Damascus near the personal home of the Syrian president are among the most important examples of the development of relations between the two countries during the past decades. The four-day visit of Hafez al-Assad to Tehran in January 1975 and signing of cooperation agreements during that trip was an example of a remarkable relationship between the two countries[90]. During this period, despite the existence of sovereign views of the two countries, there was an appropriate relationship and cooperation which was due to the existence of a common enemy called the Ba'ath regime in Iraq. Iran's support for the United Nations Security Council Resolution 316, which forced Israel to release five Syrian officers captured in Lebanon, helped to expand ties between the two countries. In 1948, in the early years of the end of the World War II the Israeli regime finds increasing power. At this point, government of Iran, unlike all the Islamic countries was the only regional supporter of this regime. In other words, at the end of World War II the Israeli regime was gaining power having support of Western countries and the Arab countries of the region with taking part in numerous battles and different oil sanctions, the Shah of Iran was the only regional supporter of the Israeli regime, and played a special role in neutralizing the sanctions and attacks of Islamic countries against the Zionist regime[91]. This view of the Islamic world and Arab countries in the region towards Tehran was pessimistic. The tipping point for these countries, especially Syria was when the Shah helped Menachem Begin (6th Prime Minister of Israel) to lead Anwar Sadat to partnership with Israel and provided the necessary measures for the Camp David Accords. A series of defeats of the Arab countries from Israel multiplied their anger towards Tehran as an ally of Tel Aviv[92]. With the start of Imam

---

[89] Ba'athist Iraq, formally the Iraqi Republic, covers the history of Iraq between 1968 and 2003, during the period of the Arab Socialist Ba'ath Party's rule.

[90] The unique relationship between Tehran and Damascus // Special website of the Supreme Leader's Representative Office in Hajj and Pilgrimage Affairs. [electronic source]. Available at: http://hajj.ir/hadjwebui/news/wfShowOpinion.aspx?id=50812 (28.10.2017)

[91] By the Zionist regime author means the Israeli regime.

[92] President Carter and the Role of Intelligence in the Camp David Accords // Jimmy Carter Presidential Library, 2013.

Khomeini's movement and a struggle against the Pahlavi regime, Syrian President Hafez al-Assad defended the Shah's opponents. Through Sayyid Musa al-Sadr[93] he communicated with the Iranian opposition factions, Mostafa Chamran and many other fighters and was responsible for training the fighting forces in his country. After the Imam's exile to Paris, Hafez al-Assad ordered all his embassies abroad, especially in Paris, not to hesitate to help the Shah's opponents. But Shah was the key to the historical relationship between Iran's revolutionaries with Syria and the Islamic Resistance Movement of Lebanon (Hezbollah[94])[95]. Many Iranian youths and students at that time studying in Europe and the United States were linked to Imam Musa Sadr due to the exile of Imam Khomeini and visited Lebanon. So that it can be said that the so-called wing of the Iranian fighters presented in Lebanon and Syria was by Imam Musa al-Sadr. This was also due to the influence and historical role of Syria in Lebanon. In other words, Syria had influence and special position in Lebanon and was very sensitive to changes in this country. Certainly, Lebanese Shiites were also counting on Syrian aid[96]. On the other hand, it was Imam Musa Sadr who considered the Alawites[97] as one of the Shiite branches, but different from other Shiites. According to Alireza Nader the Alawits are considered to be a branch of Shia religion but the importance of the role of religion in relations between Iran and Syria should not be overestimated. Although some Shiite clerics, such as the spiritual founder of Hezbollah in Lebanon Imam Musa al-Sadr recognized Alawites as the true Shiites, but complex traditions of Alawites such as lack of a single clergy or having eclectic ideas, in many spheres distinguishes them from the Shiites of Iran and Iraq[98].

However, Chamran, Ali Jannati, Mohammad Gharazi, Yahya Rahim Safavi and many others were the Iranian revolutionaries who had been in Syria with the assistance of the Syrian leaders. The Sayidda Zeinab shrine[99] in Syria was the center of the Iranian gathering and Hafez al-Assad was also

---

[electronic source]. Available at: https://www.cia.gov/library/publications/international-relations/president-carter-and-the-camp-david-accords/Carter_CampDavid_Pub.pdf (15.07.2017)

[93] Sayyid Musa al-Sadr : 4 June 1928 – disappeared in Libya on 31 August 1978) was a Lebanese-Iranian philosopher and Shi'a religious leader from a long line of distinguished clerics tracing their ancestry back to Jabal Amel.

[94] Hezbollah (Arabic: Ḥizbu 'llāh, literally "Party of Allah" or "Party of God"), also transliterated Hizbullah, Hizballah, etc.—is a Shi'a Islamist political party and militant group based in Lebanon.

[95] Taremi K. Analysis of Iranian national security policies towards the Middle East during the government of Mohammad Reza Pahlavi, 1969-1979 // Journal of the faculty of law and political science (University of Tehran), 2000.

[96] Kessler M.N., Irani G., Gubser P., Norton A. R., Chas. W., Freeman Jr. Lebanon and Syria: Internal and Regional Dimensions // Middle East Policy Council, 2001. [electronic source]. Available at: http://www.mepc.org/journal/lebanon-and-syria-internal-and-regional-dimensions (23.12.2016)

[97] The Alawis, also rendered as Alawites (Arabic: Alawīyyah), are a syncretic sect of the Twelver branch of Shia Islam, primarily centered in Syria.

[98] Schmierer R.J, Jeffrey J. F., Nader A., Nazer F. The Saudi-Iranian Rivalry and the Obama Doctrine // Middle East Policy Council, 2016. [electronic source]. Available at: http://www.mepc.org/saudi-iranian-rivalry-and-obama-doctrine-0 (22.12.2016)

[99] Sayyidah Zaynab Mosque is a mosque located in the city of Sayyidah Zaynab, in the southern suburbs of Damascus, Syria. According to Shia Muslim tradition, the mosque contains the grave of Zaynab, the daughter of ʿAlī and Fātimah

interested in the activities of the opponents of the Shah's regime and supported them. This has also darkened relations of the Shah regime and Syria. Because of the support of Syrian government, provided facilities helped using bases for training Iranian combatants. It is in these bases where Iranian revolutionaries were training with Palestinian militant groups. Based on the memories of the chief commander Yahya Rahim Safavi[100], with the support of the Syrian government, the organization has been very systematic in supporting the Iranian forces in the battle in Lebanon.

During all the years of the struggle, Imam al-Sadr and the organization under his supervision were always a place for the fighters. Some of these people were even opposed to Imam al-Sadr, but with patience all the problems of this organization were solved. He even informed Syrian President Hafez al-Assad, and he also provided different kinds of help for the fighters. Ali Jannati, a Revolutionary activist and current Iranian ambassador to Kuwait, wrote in his memory book: "One of the problems that we faced in Lebanon and Syria was the issue of residence in these countries. Our work was secret, and we could not tell anyone what we were doing. In this regard Imam Musa Sadr helped us a lot. He introduced some of the people to the Lebanese government as members of the Supreme Islamic Shia Council (in Lebanon), and thus we were able to stay officially." One of the other eyewitnesses this way describes the space of Lebanon and Syria: "... Imam Musa al-Sadr is the one who ordered the Syrian government and Hafez al-Assad to provide space and facilities to the Iranian combatants living (having residence) in that country. Many of brothers and Iranian students-combatants, who had been residing in Europe or the USA freely went to Syria without a special visa in their passports! For example, Iranian brothers who came from France to Syria, their visas were stamped on plain paper and not a passport. These were entered into the camp of the Syrian regime, under the supervision of Rifaat al-Assad... Mostafa Chamran traveled to Syria every day to talk to them... Many Iranian brothers were trained in the military camps of the Amal Movement.[101]

At a time when the Shah supported occupiers, Egypt by signing the disgraceful Camp-David Accords, set free Syria, and the Arab countries of the region in a compromise with the Zionists and the United States. The victory of the Islamic Revolution of Iran with the slogan of "Liberation of Palestine" and the destruction of Israel, gave hope for Syria and the Lebanese and Palestinian resistance forces[102]. In addition to this, the coincidence of the Islamic Revolution of Iran with the

---

and granddaughter of the Prophet Muhammad.

[100] Yahya "Rahim" Safavi , born 1952, is an Iranian military commander who served as the chief commander of the Sepah from 1 September 1997 until 1 September 2007.

[101] The Amal Movement (or Hope Movement in English, Arabic: Ḥarakat 'Amal) is a Lebanese political party associated with Lebanon's Shia community. It was co-founded by Musa al-Sadr and Hussein el Husseini as the "Movement of the Dispossessed" in 1974.

[102] Iran, Hizbullah, Hamas and the global Jihad. A new conflict paradigm for the West // Jerusalem Center for Public

failure of peace talks between Syria and Iraq has led to the popularity of the Iranian for Syrian people. All the reasons mentioned above explained why Syria welcomed the Iranian Revolution. Syria was the first Arab state to recognize the Interim Government of Iran (in general, Syria is considered the third country after the Soviet Union and Pakistan). This was also due to the common view of the two countries regarding the issues of the Islamic world[103].

Due to the declaration of solidarity of the Islamic Republic with the Palestinian issue, in the early months after the Islamic Revolution, Syria showed its interest in having strong ties with Iran. From the point of view of Syria, since the Iranian Revolution declared its solidarity with the issue of Palestine, relations with Iran were beneficial both for Syria and for the crisis of the Arab countries. On this basis, Syria and Iran were united and joined together to shorten the West's hand in the region. The hostility of Damascus to Baghdad was one of the factors contributing to the strengthening of relations between the two countries and the strategicization of relations played a major role. In other words, for Syria as it was repeatedly facing the enemies of the Shah, relations with Iran as a country of resistance were vital. In return, for Iran it was also important that it could support anti-Israeli Islamic groups, including "Hezbollah" in Lebanon and "Hamas"[104] in Palestine because this support was in fact part of the characteristic of the Islamic Revolution of Iran and should not be limited by the borders of Iran.

In another dimension, when the Islamic Revolution of Iran won, from the point of view of the autocratic countries of the region, regime supported by the East or the West fell through popular protests. This movement frightened Arab governments because majority of the Arab countries were dictatorial governments and were afraid of the revolution. At this point, Hafez al-Assad was trying to reduce the fear of these countries in the region regarding the Islamic Revolution. From the perspective of the Syrian government, with the fall of the Shah the situation of Iran was changed to the Islamic Iran; Iran of the period of the Shah, which was Iran as a friend of Israel and mercenary of the US, was destroyed and was replaced by hostility towards imperialism and Zionism.

Saudi Arabia

Iran's economic relations with Saudi Arabia and Syria before 1979 have played a crucial role in economy of the Western world[105]. Having at a disposal a quarter of the world's oil reserves, the

Affairs, 2007. [electronic source]. Available at: http://jcpa.org/wp-content/uploads/2012/08/iran-hizbullah-hamas.pdf (reference date: 01.05.2016).

[103] Barabandi B., Thompsona T.J. Friend of my Father: Iran's Manipulation of Bashar al-Assad // Atlantic Council, 2014. [electronic source]. Available at: http://www.atlanticcouncil.org/blogs/menasource/a-friend-of-my-father-iran-s-manipulation-of-bashar-al-assad (reference date: 01.05.2016).

[104] Hamas (Arabic: Ḥamās, an acronym of Ḥarakat al-Muqāwamah al-ʾIslāmiyyah Islamic Resistance Movement) is a Palestinian Sunni-Islamic fundamentalist organization.

location of the three international maritime routes (the Strait of Hormuz, the Strait of Bab-el-Mandeb (Mandeb Strait) and the Suez Canal), maritime center of Asia and Africa, a great market for economic goods and military equipment, the largest maritime border among the Arab countries, authority and influence among Arab countries and even a number of non-Arab countries of the third-world are among the factors, which the importance of Saudi Arabia and relations of this country both with the great powers and its neighbors, including Iran; the specific characteristics of Saudi Arabia and issues of regional and international level also increase the importance for some of the parties of the relationship to achieve strategic interests[106].

Review of the relations between Iran and Saudi Arabia

a) 1929-1953: In 1929 relations between the two countries began with signing of the treaty of friendship between the two countries. In 1935, embassy of Iran in Jeddah was shut down and Iranian ambassador in Cairo was elected in Saudi Arabia as an accredited ambassador. In 1943, political relations between the two countries came to a deadlock due to a bitter incident with an Iranian pilgrim Abutalib Yazdi, and these relations were cut off by Iran[107]. After that there was a ban on Hajj pilgrimage. Four years later in 1947 relations between the two countries were re-established, and in 1951, the Iranian embassy in Jeddah was once again opened.

b) 1953-1964: The nationalization of the oil industry in Iran and the Egyptian revolution in 1952 as well as the unification between Egypt and Syria in 1958 with intensifying the tensions between Iran and Egypt, turned the Shah to relations with Israel. The exchange of political representatives in 1961 was also the reason of deterioration in relations with Saudi Arabia. On the other hand, attempts to stabilize the Baghdad treaty has also led to the cooling in relations between the two governments[108].

c) 1964-1975: During this period, relations between the two countries were most influenced by major regional events and international changes, especially by the Arab-Israeli war in 1967 (The Six-Day War) and in 1973 (the Yom Kippur War), Britain's readiness to retreat from the Persian Gulf region, 1968-1971 Nixon doctrine and, finally, oil prices rising after the war in October 1973. In this period treaty on continent shelf delimitation was signed between the two countries (1968), resolving some of the disagreements over oil in the region.

---

[105]Sadat A.R. Saudi Arabia // Foundation of printing and publishing of the Ministry of Foreign Affairs. 1995.

[106] Ibid.

[107] Kamali H.R. Iran and Saudi Arabia: Past and Future // Iran Review, 2014. [electronic source]. Available at: http://www.iranreview.org/content/Documents/Iran-and-Saudi-Arabia-Past-and-Future.htm (reference date: 02.10.2016).

[108] Lahouti A. United States of America and security of the Persian Gulf // Magazine of political and economic information.

d) 1975-1979: Among the most significant changes in this period, that has been effective in changing relations between the two countries, can be mentioned the resolution of the border disputes between the two countries in 1975, the death of Faisal bin Abdulaziz Al Saud and its impact on duration of the Tehran-Riyadh cooperation in the shadow of good neighborhood. Finally, it includes the emphasis of non-entry into the treaties by Saudi Arabia and the Gulf states, during the Foreign Ministers' Conference of the Persian Gulf, Saudi Arabia, Iraq and Iran in Muscat city in 1967[109].

e) 1979-1999: With the victory of the Islamic Revolution in Iran, Khalid bin Abdulaziz Al Saud said that the establishment of the Islamic Government in Iran would be the introduction of closer intercourse between the two countries, but the establishment of the Liberation Front in Tehran and holding of the first Hajj by Iranian Hajjaj gradually led to a public opposition of Saudi Arabia. The Islamic Republic officials also criticized Saudi policies toward the issues of the region, the Islamic world and its close relationship with the United States. Saudi Arabia was also giving a shelter for the US spies and military advisers, as well as anti-revolutionaries who escaped from Iran.

A few months after the start of the Iran-Iraq war in 1980, in order to create a defensive barrier against the influence of the Iranian revolution in the region, in particular the prevention of internal uprisings and the suppression of liberation movements in the region, as well as the expansion of the influence of Riyadh on other neighbors, and in the same time elimination of Iran from being gendarme of the region, cooperation in the economic and political fields with other countries, The Cooperation Council for the Arab States of the Gulf was created. It included such countries as Saudi Arabia, Kuwait, Emirate, Oman, Qatar and Bahrain. Beginning of the Iran-Iraq war in 1980 with the support and encouragement of Iraq from Saudi Arabia ended up with hostility in relations between Iran and Saudi Arabia.[110]

Saudi Arabia encouraged Iraq to start war with Iran and supported Hussein's hometown of up to 30 billion dollars during the war. Following the increase in Saudi Arabia's oil production, due to the lack of oil in Iran and Iraq in the oil market, and by adopting the same approach by the Emirates, Kuwait and then Qatar, Iran issued a statement to protect its oil wells declaring that if Saudi Arabia or other Persian Gulf country would support Iraq, then the battlefield will extend to these areas[111]. Saudi Arabia also extracted 280,000 barrels of oil a day from the neutral area and sold it to Iraq.

---

[109] The Kings Of The Kingdom. King AbdulAziz bin AbdulRahman bin Faisal Al Saud (1876 – 1953) // Ministry of Commerce and Investment. [electronic source]. Available at: http://mci.gov.sa/en/AboutKingdom/Pages/KingdomKings.aspx (reference date: 02.10.2016).
[110] Iran-Iraq war. [electronic source]. Available at: https://www.saylor.org/site/wp-content/uploads/2011/08/HIST351-11.1.4-Iran-Iraq-War.pdf (reference date: 01.05.2016).
[111] Homayun B. Secret relations between the United States and Saudi Arabia (weapon-oil-Iran-Iraq) // Magazine of political and economic information.

Every day between 300 and 500 barrels of oil would pass the Iraq's land. Part of the Iraqi arms purchasers which was delayed, was taken under its responsibility and many ports and its airports were fully provided for the transportation of the goods and military supplies required by the Iraqi Army.

With the martyrdom of about 400 Iranian pilgrims by the Saudi security forces in Mecca in July 1987, deterioration of relations reached its peak. Eight months later, in April 1988, Saudi Arabia unilaterally finished its relations with the Islamic Republic and delayed the Iranian diplomats who resided there for a week to leave Saudi Arabia. Suspending of relations lasted for about three years and during this time Iranians were deprived of participation in the Hajj[112] ceremony[113].

f)   1999-2002: In this period, transnational factors and international changed played the most important role not only in relations between the two countries of Iran and Saudi Arabia, but also in the Persian Gulf region, the Middle East and even the world.

In 1989, during the beginning of the period under discussion, the U.S. strategy in the Persian Gulf had reached the desired outcome of the government: the Soviet Union had left Afghanistan, and most importantly, from the point of view of the USA, for a while, there was no danger from the Iranian side and the Soviet Union to the Persian Gulf; in short, the United States had reached its three basic goals: putting pressure on Iran, securing the Persian Gulf region, and getting full access to oil resources and security of the flow of oil. On the other hand, the specific way that ended the war between Iran and Iraq had led to a shift in Saudi Arabia's approach; because foreign help pushed Iraq to conclude a truce, as a result, Iraq claimed to have a psychological victory. Then the danger of Iraq grew larger than Iran, and the ambitions of Saddam Hussein and his powerful army became more important than anything else[114].

During the period between 1990 and 2000 Saudi Arabia, being the third largest oil producer in the world and first in OPEC[115], payed an attention to getting more access to energy resources, the supply of free flow of oil and the limitation of the range of influence of competitors. It also played a

---

[112] The Hajj (/hædʒ/;Arabic: Ḥaǧǧ "pilgrimage") is an annual Islamic pilgrimage to Mecca, the most holy city for Muslims, and a mandatory religious duty for Muslims that must be carried out at least once in their lifetime by all adult Muslims who are physically and financially capable of undertaking the journey, and can support their family during their absence.

[113] 400 die as Iranian marchers battle Saudi police in Mecca; embassies smashed in Teheran // The New York Times, 1987. [electronic source]. Available at: http://www.nytimes.com/1987/08/02/world/400-die-iranian-marchers-battle-saudi-police-mecca-embassies-smashed-teheran.html?pagewanted=all (reference date: 03.10.2016).

[114] Dehshiyar Hossein, US Foreign Policy in Asia, Tehran, Abrar Moaser, Azar 2003.

[115] Organization of the Petroleum Exporting Countries (OPEC, /ˈoʊpɛk/ OH-pek, or OPEP in several other languages) is an intergovernmental organization of 14 nations as of May 2017, founded in 1960 in Baghdad by the first five members (Iran, Iraq, Kuwait, Saudi Arabia, Venezuela), and headquartered since 1965 in Vienna.

key role in the political agenda of the U.S. Also, Saudi Arabia's unique role among Arab and Islamic countries and its strategic position would make friendship with this country very important for the United States. In one TV discussion, which came out in 1993 an American oil analyst Edwin Rothschild says: "America's excessive reliance on oil of Saudi Arabia will increase every day, and this will be dangerous to our national security"[116].

During the nineties, the Saudis gradually approached Iran, herewith maintaining good relations with the Americans. From this approach, there are possibilities of regulation of Iran by peaceful means[117]. From another point of view, Iran has also tended to expand its ties with Saudi Arabia. Thus, expanding of relations had reached to the point when in February 1998 Hashemi Rafsanjani visited Saudi Arabia and got a warm reception from Abdullah bin Abdulaziz Al Saud and met other princes. He also headed the pilgrimage of the Iranian delegation from Jannat al-Baqi' cemetery[118] in Medina. These relations, including often visits of high ranking officials of the two countries and national company of Abdullah bin Abdulaziz Al Saud during the Summit of Islamic countries in Tehran, opened a new chapter. But there is no doubt that the most important event of this period is the incident of September 11, 2001 and the participation of 11 Saudi citizens in this terrorist attack. The bombings at the World Trade Center in 1993, the destruction of the U.S. embassies in Tanzania and Kenya in 1998, the attack on the Khobar Towers[119] in Saudi Arabia in 1996 and the attack on the U.S. Navy on the coast of Yemen, were events that confronted the U.S. interests and the September 11 attacks completed this confrontation.[120]

These events clearly strengthened positions and views, which considered supplying, maintaining the security and stability of the Persian Gulf and the Middle East linked directly to the establishment of sustainable reforms and democracies in the countries of the region. In the same time big actors in the international arena, especially the United States simply ignored the internal crisis in the region (suppression of dissenters, human rights abuses, increasing administrative and economic corruption, etc.) before the events took place. To provide energy security in the region

---

[116] The arming of Saudi Arabia, 1993. [electronic source]. Available at: http://s3.amazonaws.com/911timeline/1990s/frontline0121693.html (reference date: 14.10.2016).
[117] Jones P. Towards a regional security regime for the Middle East // Stockholm International Peace Research Institute (SIPRI), 1998. [electronic source]. Available at: https://www.files.ethz.ch/isn/96416/1998_12_SIPRI98Jones.pdf (reference date: 14.10.2016).
[118] Jannat al-Baqi' (Arabic translit:. Jannat al-Baqī', lit. 'Garden of Baqi') is a cemetery in Medina, present-day Saudi Arabia, located to the southeast of the Masjid al-Nabawi (The Prophet's Mosque).
[119] The Khobar Towers bombing was a terrorist attack on part of a housing complex in the city of Khobar, Saudi Arabia, located near the national oil company (Saudi Aramco) headquarters of Dhahran and nearby King Abdulaziz Air Base on June 25, 1996.
[120] Significant Terrorist Incidents, 1961-2003: A Brief Chronology // U.S. Department of State archives. [electronic source]. Available at: https://2001-2009.state.gov/r/pa/ho/pubs/fs/5902.htm (reference date: 14.10.2016).

there was a special relationship with countries and Arab governments, especially Saudi Arabia. The golden age of relations between Washington and Riyadh after the September 11 attacks turned into a nightmare of distrust and suspicion for both sides. In new conditions the U.S. was making Egypt follow the comprehensive reforms based on western development models and structural changes in regional governments. However, providing such reforms, as it is previewed in the first plan of "the Greater Middle East", could have led to the changes of the foundations of power and legitimacy of Saudi Arabia, as well as the other traditional regional governments. The September 11 attacks clearly influenced relations between Iran and Saudi Arabia. The efforts of Saudi Arabia rebuild the U.S. lost confidence once again, led Riyadh away from Tehran. This country even welcomed "the sharp literature", that the mass media and the USA officials used against Iran after the 11/9 attacks. After these terrorist attacks they pointed with finger to Iran and turned growing international pressure to reforms inside the country[121].

Conclusion of the first chapter

The first part of the first chapter explains the legal and political structure of foreign policy of the Islamic Republic of Iran. It is noticed that the government's decisions in the field of foreign policy, in its majority, follow the national interests. The second part of the chapter examines economic, cultural, security and military aspects. The author concludes that Iran is an important actor in the Middle East region due to its history, economic development, history and geopolitical meaning. The constructive role of Iran is evident because any instability or insecurity, lack of social, political and economic progress in the region, first of all, compromise the national interests of Iran. In other words, it is the regional development that responds to the national interests of Iran. Due to these characteristics, the Islamic Republic of Iran can play a constructive role in implementing the great Middle East plan, including political development and democratization, economic progress, as well as social development and progress. But Iran's support for such plans, above all, requires the granting of a proper regional role to Iran and its status. In the last part of this chapter the author studies Iran's relations with Saudi Arabia and Syria before the 1979 revolution. It can be concluded that in that period Iran and Saudi Arabia were a part of the strategy and politics of friendship of Nixon, which meant providing the U.S. interests in the Middle East. Iran's relations with Syria were quite cold because of the Shah's support of Israel and the Syria's support of the opponents of the Shah[122].

---

[121] Asadi S. Effective variables in Foreign Policy of Saudi Arabia // Foreign Policy Quarterly, 2011.

[122] Mohammad Reza Pahlavi (26 October 1919 – 27 July 1980), known as Mohammad Reza Shah (Persian), was the

Chapter 2. Characteristics of Iran's foreign policy in the Middle East during the leadership of Imam Khomeini (1979-1989)

2.1. Islamization of foreign policy

With the Islamic Revolution of Iran, the Islamic dimension of Islamic foreign policy was highlighted. Attitude of Mehdi Mazagran when was to serve Iran through Islam and Imam Khomeini's idea was to serve Islam through Iran better reflect this situation.[123] After the revolution, Iran's foreign policy was largely based on Islamic values and was changed according to Islamic guidelines. After the revolution, the whole manner of Tehran became more intense in the first years after the revolution and during the imposed Iran-Iraq war.[124]

To understand Iran's foreign policy, the "political Islam" must be studied. The background of this approach in Iran dates to the early 1960s, when Ayatollah Khomeini opposed policies of Mohammad Reza Pahlavi. After the Islamic Revolution in Iran in 1979, Islamists took over the government. In the first decade of the establishment of the Islamic Republic, Islamic interests dominated all aspects of Iran's political life. This attitude did not fit into the accepted norms of international behavior and it was hard to distinguish between Iranian foreign and domestic politics.[125] Since then, Islam has always played a major role in Iran's foreign policy, and still explains the goals of this country and ways of reaching it.[126]

In fact, in the diplomatic relations of the Islamic Republic of Iran, there are four important historical periods: November 4, 1979 (Aban 13, 1358), which is Iran hostage crisis[127]; September 22, 1980, when Iraq invaded Iran (Shahrivar 31, 1359); July 17 (Mordad 6, 1368), when Iran accepted Resolution 598[128][129]; and July 28, 1989, when Hashemi Rafsanjani was elected as the

---

last Shah of Iran from 16 September 1941 until his overthrow by the Iranian Revolution on 11 February 1979.

[123] Bazargan M. Iran's Revolution in two Movements // Tehran publisher, 1981-82.

[124] Graham E. Fuller. The center of the universe: The geopolitics of Iran (Rand Corporation Research Study) // Orbis, 1992.

[125] Wilfram F.Hanrieder. Compatibility and Consensus: A Proposal for the Conceptual Linking of External and Internal Dimensions of Foreign Policy // American Political Science Review, 1965.

[126] Wilfarm E Hanrieder, Foregn Policies and the International System: A Theoretical International // New York: General Learning Press, 1971.

[127] The Iran hostage crisis was a diplomatic standoff between Iran and the United States. Fifty-two American diplomats and citizens were held hostage for 444 days from November 4, 1979, to January 20, 1981 after a group of Iranian students belonging to the Muslim Student Followers of the Imam's Line, who supported the Iranian Revolution, took over the U.S. Embassy in Tehran. It stands as the longest hostage crisis in recorded history.

[128] THE SITUATION BETWEEN IRAN AND IRAQ // UN [electronic source]. Available at: https://peacemaker.un.org/sites/peacemaker.un.org/files/IQ%20IR_870720_Security%20Council%20Resolution%20598%20%281987%29.pdf (reference date: 07.08.2017).

[129] United Nations Security Council resolution 598 S/RES/0598 (1987), (UNSC resolution 598) adopted unanimously on

president, and Iran's policy entered a new stage. It can be said that "the second period of the Islamic Republic" [130]began one year later after the adoption of Resolution 598. [131]

Iran's foreign policy during the Iran's interim government of Mehdi Bazargan[132] was not clear and sometimes followed the policies of the previous government. The Bagargan policy can be seen as ordinary, moderate, without regional ambitions but at the same time a policy protecting the country's independence and territorial integrity. However, to some extent, this policy followed, the principle of "Neither East, nor West" in the sense of non-commitment to both superpowers in the bipolar system of the international community.[133]Oppositely to the militant Islam, a new order based on non-traditional idealism was promised. The U.S. embassy hostage crisis, which Imam Khomeini, leader of the Islamic Revolution called a "bigger revolution than the first one", was carried out by "students following the line of the Imam" on the same basis. This was the first major action taken by the revolutionary forces[134]. This event had two implications for the internal affairs of Iran and the international community, which resulted in the short term. First, the Bazargan government, which suffered from numerous centers of power, one day resigned. His resignation meant the complete dissolution of Iranians from past politics and the beginning of radicalism in Iran's foreign policy. Second, an eight-year with Iraq had just begun.

During the passing away of Khomeini (Mordad 14, 1368) he changed the path of economic and national reconstruction of Iran, there was a review of Iran's foreign policy foundation.

First stage: Islamization of foreign policy

The Islamic Revolution of Iran is described in the preamble to the Constitution of the Islamic Republic: "The revolution is a movement for the victory of the oppressed ... against the oppressors ... inside and outside Iran. In particular, the revolution is on the international level and in helping other Islamic and popular movements to strengthen the resistance of the oppressed people and the world Ummah unity.[135] Imam Khomeini also explained this concept on September 3, 1983 (Shahrivar 12, 1362) saying: "To counter the propaganda of the so-called nationalist and

---

20 July 1987, after recalling Resolution 582 and 588, called for an immediate ceasefire between Iran and Iraq and the repatriation of prisoners of war, and for both sides to withdraw to the international border.

[130] Mossad A. M. Nouvelle orientation de la deuxieme republique iranienne: priorites-instrument-contraintes in Crise du golfe et ordre politique au Moyen- Orient (The crisis of Gulf and the Middle Eastern political order), edited by Micheal Camau, A.E. Hilal Dessouki, and J. C. Vatin // Paris: CNRS, 1993.

[131] Djalili M.R. Iran-Iraq: radioscopie dune guerre ambigue, (Iran-Iraq: radioscopy of an ambiguous war) // Politique Internationale, 1983.

[132] Mehdi Bazargan ; (1 September 1907 – 20 January 1995) was an Iranian scholar, academic, long-time pro-democracy activist and head of Iran's interim government, making him Iran's first prime minister after the Iranian Revolution of 1979.

[133] Bazargan M. Iran's Revolution in two Movements // Tehran publisher, 1981-82

[134] Leeden M., Levis W. Debacle: The American 3 Fallure in Iran // New York: Knopf, 1980.

[135] Preamble, Op.cit.

westernized people that prevent Muslims from defending their rights, the only way is the unity of the Muslims, and more important than that is the unity of the oppressed people of the world." These words had a clear regional and international impact on Iran. This issue, more than anything else, calls for a permanent revolution of the people. Article 152 of the Constitution of Iran states: "The foreign policy of the Islamic Republic of Iran is based upon the rejection of all forms of domination, both the exertion of it and submission to it, the preservation of the independence of the country in all respects and its territorial integrity, the defense of the rights of all Muslims, non-alignment with respect to the hegemonist superpowers, and the maintenance of mutually peaceful relations with all non-belligerent States." Article 154 of the same Constitution[136] states the following: "The Islamic Republic of Iran has as its ideal human felicity throughout human society, and considers the attainment of independence, freedom, and rule of justice and truth to be the right of all people of the world. Accordingly, while scrupulously refraining from all forms of interference in the internal affairs of other nations, it supports the just struggles of the mustad'afun (oppressed) against the mustakbirun (oppression) in every corner of the globe." The Constitution does not explain how these two opposing goals come together. The principle of non-interference in the internal affairs of these countries does not allow a state to support the oppressed people of another country[137]. While, according to Iranian leaders, the defense of the rights of all oppressors creates a great responsibility for the Islamic Republic, because ideological and Islamist interests have priority over national interests. Over the next few years, all actions and resources were spent on this idea, and even the imposition of war on the part of Iraq could not change the views of the supporters of this perspective.

In the first decade of the establishment of the Islamic Republic, a specific political system was adopted and a new policy was announced; the discontinuation of diplomatic relations with the "aggressor Israel" on February 18, 1979 (Bahman 23, 1357)-less than a week after the revolution - the discontinuation of relations with the white minority ruling South Africa on March 14 (Esfand, 23), the same year as the official abolition of Iran's membership of the Central Treaty Organization in March 13, 1979 (Esfand, 22 1357) and the interruption of diplomatic relations with Egypt on April 30, 1979 (Ordibehesht 10, 1358) were the priorities of the new Islamic government of Iran. The support of the left-wing parties from the message of the Supreme Leader of the Islamic Revolution shows that they also confirmed the logic of these ideological and militant tendencies.

---

[136] Article 154, Op. cit.
[137] Bazargan's interview with Oriana Fallaci // The New Yorker, 1979.

From the perspective of these groups, the international law and international institutions seeking to establish multilateral relations serve the interests of the great powers. [138]

Despite the formation of these tendencies, Islamism desires were not realized. The situation was aggravated by the lack of political experience and efficient military regime, as well as the hostility and suspicion of many foreign powers caused the Islamic Republic to face international constraints. This situation had consequences and limited the country on the international level. It also did not condemn Iraq's aggression in a serious way. Iranian leaders considered that such an aggression was the result of a conspiracy of conservative Arab governments and support of the Western powers.

Imam Khomeini and Islamization of foreign policy

Without the study of Imam Khomeini's thinking this foreign policy is not possible. He was the one who put the Islamic paradigm into the foreign policy of Iran and then highlighted its Islamic dimension. During the Islamic Revolution, two strategic slogans: "Independence, liberty, Islamic Republic" and "Neither East nor West, the Islamic Republic" helped to spread the new ideas in the nation and the Iranian elites. These ideas, which were deeply religious in its nature were the result of the Imam's religious character and had a deep religious structure in the Iranian nation, which led to the withdrawal of Iran from the closed circle of a bipolar world and a rise to new horizons, based on national dignity, national interests, human rights and mutual respect according to the Islamic teachings.[139] In fact, this process also outlines the goals of foreign policy of the Islamic Republic of Iran, creating an Islamic society based on "Islame Nabe Mohammadi" (pure Islam of Mohammad), confrontation with Israel and the West, especially the United States, defending Muslims and liberation movements.[140]

Before entering the discussion of the principles, base and goals of foreign policy from the point of view of Imam Khomeini, let's take a closer look at this concept.

Basics, principles and goals

About the basics there must be said that the main role in decision making lies in the foundations, intellectual structure and beliefs of the political personalities and politicians. In fact, the types of governments and the bases of their legitimacy differentiate the basis and behavior of their

---

[138] Mofid K. The cost of the Iran-Iraq war has been estimated at $1.097 billion. The Economic Consequences of the Gulf War // New York: Routlefge, 1990.

[139]Foreign policy and international relations in the viewpoint of Imam Khomeini // Tehran: Institute for publishing works f Imam Khomeini Works, 2002.

[140] Sariolghalam M. Foreign policy of the Islamic Republic of Iran: theoretical review and coalition paradigm // Tehran: Strategic Research Center, 2000.

foreign policy actions, as well as its internal politics. In the context of a "goal", it is said that the entry of any state in the global arena is based on its goals and motives. The goals outside of the of the government borders reflect the needs and origins of the actors of foreign policy and the perceptions derived from the facts surrounding it. Here the goals are intended to be the goal of foreign policy.[141]

Principles of foreign policy from the point of view of Imam Khomeini

Considering the fact that Imam Khomeini was a religious leader with a political thought based on Islam, the principles had the basis of particular Islam, including the book and the Sunna. In fact, the structure of foreign policy is based on the commitment to holy sharia[142]. Therefore, moral values and reasons form the basis of Imam Khomeini's foreign policy. Of course, it should be mentioned that Islam and religion cannot be considered exclusively the morality of Imam Khomeini. Emphasizing on the human and ethical content of the revolution, he states: "The content of this revolution, Islam and Islamic ethics, human ethics and the cultivation of human beings have been based on humanity."[143]

It does not mean that the Islamic Republic of Iran should be reformed with a government that has no belief in Islam and in the ethics of humanity. For further explanation it should be noticed that, for example, the basis of the principle of defending the oppressed in foreign policy in the eyes of the Imam is the Holy Qur'an.

Principles of Islamic government foreign policy as seen by Imam Khomeini

Principles of foreign policy can provide behavioral framework necessary to the agents of the Islamic system, and adherence to these principles is a way of distinguishing the Islamic Iran from other governments. Indeed, the Islamic Republic government functions based on specific principles to achieve its goals. The principles of foreign policy provided by Imam Khomeini can be considered as one of the official sources of decision making in the policy of the Islamic Republic of Iran. In such a way that even the new leader of the Islamic Revolution has stated that the general line in the policy of the Islamic Republic of Iran is the same as the one described by Imam Khomeini.[144] In fact, unique characteristics and qualities of Imam Khomeini, such as foolishness, courage,

---

[141] Haghighat S. S. Confluence Theory & Religious Leadership Theory // Mofid University, Qom, Iran, 2017. [electronic source]. Available at: http://www.mofidu.ac.ir/_DouranPortal/Documents/C.V._ENGLISH_%20_2__20170730_080041.pdf (reference date: 02.11.2017).

[142] Sharia, Sharia law, or Islamic law is the religious law forming part of the Islamic tradition. It is derived from the religious precepts of Islam, particularly the Quran and the Hadith.

[143] Ibid.

[144] Izadi B. On the foreign policy of the Islamic Republic of Iran // Qom: book boostan, 1992.

uncompromisingness, decisiveness, purity and mysticism, were such that he had created a powerful role for himself, and this leadership role in how to adopt decisions in the internal and external dimensions played an important role[145]. Let's look at the principles of foreign policy from Imam Khomeini's point of view:

Principle of exporting revolution. The export of the revolution is one of the important issues of the Imam, which means exporting the experience of the Islamic Revolution to other countries of the world. From Imam Khomeini's point of view, the purpose of exporting a revolution is the same as the expansion of Islam. Considering this, Imam Khomeini believes: We end the dominance and oppression of our hostile countries by exporting our revolution, which is, in fact, the issuance of true pure Islam and the expression of Mohammadi's pure sentences.[146] From his point of view in order to overcome the difficulties, people must stand against all powers and exert human values from here to the rest of the world. Indeed, according to him, export of the revolution is cultural. On the export of the Iranian revolution, Rouhollah Ramezani states: "The emergence of the export of the revolution is a fundamental pillar in foreign policy, and just like the Iranian revolution itself, it reflects the internal political dynamics of Iran." [147] In fact, from the beginning, the main goal of Iranian foreign policy was the revolutionary propagation of Islam; this goal comes from the work of the Qur'an for Muslims in order to realize and propagate the divine message throughout the universe. In another passage Rouhollah Ramezani claims that Imam Khomeini's demand for the exporting revolution is in his ideology and the political Iran-Islamic culture.[148] Imam Khomeini says the following about the export of the revolution: "We must extort the world with the greatest intensity of our revolution and abandon this idea that we are not able to export the revolution; because Islam does not distinguish between Islamic countries. We are the protectors of all the disadvantaged. All the super powers and all other powers have come to destroy us. If we stay in a limited space, we will, for sure, fall.[149] We are exporting our revolution to the whole world, because our revolution is Islamic, and until there is no god but God; Muhammad is the messenger of God" spread throughout the world, there is a struggle, and we are going to fight anywhere in the world against the arrogant."[150] Of course, he reminds us to avoid the misuse of the meaning of the export of revolution and the

[145] Haghighat S. Transnational responsibilities in Islamic Republic foreign Policy // Tehran: Presidential Strategic Research Center, 1997.

[146] In search of the way of the words of the Imam (tenth workbook) // Tehran: Amir Kabir, 1983-1984.

[147] Esposito J. The Iranian revolution and its global reflection, translation by Doctor Shanechi M.M. Article issuing the Iranian revolution: politics, objectives and instruments, Ramezani R.K. // Tehran: Center for the recognition of Islam and Iran, 2003.

[148] Ibid.

[149] Ibid.

[150] Message from Imam on the occasion of the anniversary of the bloody Mecca incident, 1988.

negative perceptions: "We say that our revolution must be exported everywhere, and we do not want any misunderstandings such as changing the borders; all countries must stay in their own place. We want that what happened in Iran happen in all countries and nations and "cut the hands" of the superpowers. The meaning of exporting a revolution is to wake up all nations and all governments and save themselves from this plight"[151]. According to the above, it can be concluded that the export of revolution from the point of view of Imam Khomeini is the export of Islam Nabe Mohammadi (pure Islam of Mohammad), which is one of the missions and obligations of the Islamic Republic. As a result, the support of the underprivileged and oppressed nations and the support of the Islamic world's government in this regard finds its concept and meaning. "Our logic, the logic of Islam, is that no one but you should dominate over yourself. You should not be dominated. We also do not want to be dominated."[152]

He mentions the program of foreign policy of Iran as a program of Islam and states:" We are ready to defend Islam and the Islamic countries and the independence of Islamic countries anyway. Our program is the program of Islam, the total unity of the Muslims, the union of Islamic countries..."[153]And in another passage, it is necessary to mention defending all Muslims: "We do not mean one country, the country of Iran, we consider all Islamic countries as ours, as us, it must definitely be that way. We call for the defense of all Muslims." Imam admits that Islam is for everyone and compassionate for humanity, and we are all subordinate to Islam and compassionate for the same values. The Iranian nation does not allow any nation to interfere in its internal affairs, Iran maintains its freedom and independence, and will interact with all countries in a similar way[154]. When the journalist of Times (the U.S.) asks him: "What will the foreign policy of the Islamic Republic be in general? Imam replies: "The Islamic Republic of Iran has good relations with all the countries and believes in mutual respect, if others also believe in a mutual respect". Referring to the teachings of the Prophets, Imam Khomeini considered the nation of Islam to follow a statement that summarizes its program in two words: "Do not oppress, do not be under the oppression; and you shall not be wronged"[155]. In his statement to the Ambassadors on February 11, 1980, Imam Khomeini stated: "We will not oppress, nor will we be oppressed." In fact, the Imam wants to

---

[151] Ibid.
[152]Imam Khomeini's statement on the Shah's mission to implement colonial, economic-cultural plans, 1978.
[153]Imam Khomeini's statements in among of all ambassadors, 1984.
[154] Ayatollah Khamenei's Opinion on Unity
[electronic source]. Available at:
http://english.khamenei.ir/Opinions/tunity (reference date: 01.11.2017).
[155] Swenson E. What Happens When Islamists Take Power? The Case of Iran, 2005.
[electronic source]. Available at:
http://gemsofislamism.tripod.com/khomeini_promises_kept.html (reference date: 01.11.2017).

oppose superpowers and oppressors. He considered the compromise with the tyrant to be harassment to the oppressed contrary to the prophets' principles: "Under the leadership of the Prophet Muhammad, we call these two words; we are not tyrant and not oppressors ..." [156]

The principle of Neither East nor West, which was, in fact, one of the main slogans of the people in the midst of the revolution is derived from the words of Imam Khomeini, who have referred to this issue in many cases: "The Iranian people, without relying on the West and the East, will stand on their feet and rely on their religious and national capital." [157] In another way, this slogan is referred as following: "What the young people call as "Nether East not West" means that no one may interfere in Iran, and this is perfectly right".[158]

Indeed, he is looking for a free and independent Islamic Government that does not rely on the orientation towards the West or the East and the balance of power in this region of the world is preserved. Foreign policy objectives from Imam Khomeini's point of view:

Independence. Despite international pressure and internal crises, this principle did not mean isolating Iran. Imam Khomeini was constantly emphasizing the real privacy of Iranians and their rights and their dignity. Indeed, political independence is one of the principles providing the dignity of the Islamic community. According to Imam Khomeini the roots of damage to independence, cultural thought, and the greatest dependence of the oppressed nations on the superpowers is an intellectual and internal affinity, and that other dependencies originated from it. He considered the solution to achieving the goal of gaining intellectual independence and getting rid of dependence in identifying effective national cultural achievements. The greatest disaster for our nation was considered to be intellectual dependence that we suppose that everything comes from the West and that we are poor in all aspects and that we must import it from the outside.[159]

Of course, when speaking of independence in the foreign policy of a country, independence means the three stages of policy, decision-making and implementation of a decision that appears in the political, cultural, economic, defense and other fields. Although it may seem that political independence is important, but from the perspective of the Imam, cultural independence is even more important. [160] Therefore, in order to achieve independence, self-centeredness of thought and self-discovery must be achieved. Imam Khomeini in this regard states: "Basically, the belief in these two things: the belief in weakness and disability. And the belief in the power and the ability of the

---

[156] Ibid.
[157]Interview of Imam Khomeini with the Unita newspaper, the Organ of the communist party of Italy, 1983.
[158] Ibid.
[159]Ghazizadeh K. Islamic jurisprudential and political ideas of Imam Khomeini // Tehran: Presidential center of strategic studies, 1998.
[160] Sotoudeh M. Imam Khomeini and theoretical foundations of foreign policy // Political science quarterly, 1999.

nation to find a way so that we can stand against great powers".[161] Of course, he did not overlook the economic dependence that led to political affiliation. In relation to economic dependence, he also said: "Your work and your activism save your country from dependence in addition to the material and spiritual values which are available to you".[162]

Responding to a question of one journalist who asked Imam of what the foreign policy of the Islamic Republic would be, especially in relation to the superpowers, he said: "The policy of the Islamic Government, the preservation of independence, the freedom of the nation, the government and the country, as well as mutual respect after independence, when there will not be any difference between superpowers and non-superpowers." Finally, Imam considers the continuation of political, social, economic, and security independence of the country as dependent on the military and police forces, and they are considered as the pillar of the independence of the country[163].

Unity of the Islamic Ummah. He considered the unity between Muslims and oppressed people and other Islamic countries and called on the leaders of Islamic countries to have a monotheistic word against the foreign enemy: "Muslims of the world, and oppressed ones, rise and defend your religion and destiny, and do not be afraid of luck of power"[164]. From Imam Khomeini's point of view, in order to free the detainees from corruption and enjoy a decent human life, there must be a support of one another and limit the power of the arrogant. In this way, Iran's policy is to support such movements: "The Islamic Republic of Iran will be with you and along with all Muslims, as well as with all the oppressed people of the world." [165] In relation to helping the liberation movements of the world, he says: "The free Iranian nation supports the oppressed nations of the world against those whose logic is their balloon, tanks and their slogans…We support all liberation movements around the world who are fighting in the cause of God, truth and freedom."[166] And in other paths he also mentions supporting these movements until they reach the level of the free society: "Again, I reaffirm all the liberation movements of the world and hope that they will succeed in achieving their free society and the Islamic Republic would assist them when it is needed." [167] In relation peaceful coexistence, Imam Khomeini states: "We treat all governments with

[161] Ibid.
[162] Ibid.
[163]Mir-Khalili S.J. Imam Khomeini's Viewpoints on Iranian Foreign Policy// Iran Review, 2008. [electronic source]. Available at: http://www.iranreview.org/content/Documents/Imam_Khomeini%E2%80%99s_Viewpoints_on_Iranian_Foreign_Policy.htm (reference date: 01.06.2016).
[164]Message from Imam Khomeini on the occasion of the holy and martyrdom, 1981.
[165] Meeting with the members of the Center Council of Lebanese Hezbollah, 1987.
[166] Message from Imam Khomeini on the occasion of the birth and procession of Prophet Muhammad, 1980.
[167] Message from Imam on the occasion of the second anniversary of the victory of the revolution, 1981.

tolerance and we never want to deal with violence ...."[168] He talks about peace and peaceful coexistence between the nations of the world: "We want peace. We want peace with all the people of the world. We want to have peaceful coexistence with the whole world. We want to live among the people of the world."[169]

Referring to the fact that we are good with the nations, he said: "Relations between nations should be based on spiritual/moral issues, and in this regard, the distance does not affect the case, as a country may be a neighbor but does not have needed spiritual relation. Our relations with countries will be based on the principles of Islam". It should be noted that the foreign policy of the Islamic Republic has bases that affect the principles and goals. First of all, we have to establish the principles and objectives of the transnational responsibilities proving the principles and objectives of these responsibilities. But it should be noted that the cases of interference are low, and even in these few cases, there can be some compromise between the principles and the goals. Foreign policy has always been the most controversial field of policy. In this field, there are various factors which have influence in the Islamic Revolution of Iran, where Imam Khomeini has a special place in explaining the principles of foreign policy. What is important is that Islam became a paradigm in foreign policy, and Iran's foreign policy became Islamist. In fact, according to Imam, what was said about the bases, principles, and intentions was drawn in Iran's foreign policy: independence, the export of revolution, the unity of the Islamic Ummah, respect for mutual rights, the negation of oppression, the principle of disbelieving against Muslims in any field, including political, social, cultural, economic and military, the good and peaceful coexisting relations with others, the defense of Islam and Muslims, the policy of the Neither East nor West, the expansion of relations on the basis of Islamic and humanitarian principles and as well as help and assistance to the liberation movements. In relation to each of these cases, it is an example of Imam Khomeini's sayings, and perhaps it can be acknowledged that, in some cases, his view goes beyond the existing structure and international law. Including his reading of Islam that considered "Islame Nabe Mohammadi" (pure Islam of Mohammad).

In general it can be said that during the first years after the Revolution, Iranian foreign policy was Islamized, the term which can be used in order to describe the new priorities, such as unity with the whole Islamic Ummah, independence, the slogan "Neither East not West", which describes the new vector in the best way. Iran was aiming to reach a goal of independent foreign policy choices based on mutual respect.

---

[168]Imam Khomeini's statement in a group of personnel of the Ministry of Roads & Urban Development, 1984.
[169] Imam Khomeini's statements in the words of Sayyid Ali Khamenei , 1986.

2.2. Priorities of Iran's foreign policy (governments of Bazargan and Mousavi)

Iran's foreign policy went through a change after the revolution. Oil, energy, support of the allies, the Nixon doctrine[170] and "the so-called periphery states" according to Ben Gurion's theory[171] were Iran's priority in the previous regime. After the revolution, these priorities paying attention to the post-revolutionary government can be described as followings:

Priorities of foreign policy of the Islamic Republic of Iran

Realistic discourse (1978-1981) Government of Bazargan

The foreign policy of the Islamic Republic of Iran, as well as the foreign policy of other countries, has been influenced by the changes and transformation of one of the foreign policy dialogues. The foreign policy of the Bazargan government is one of the most controversial periods in Iran's foreign policy history, based on the principle of non-alignment and the principle of "Neither East nor the West". In the multiple writings on the review of foreign policy of Iran, starting from the era of the interim government was seen as the era of pragmatic discourse (expediency oriented) or realism. This period begins with the prime minister Bazargan and the interim government and ends with the occupation of the U.S. Embassy by students following the Imam's line and Mehdi Bazargan's resignation.[172] During the very first days of power, Bazargan declared that Iran would pursue a policy based on the principle of non-alignment. It was a strategic policy that was invented by the world leaders in developing countries to pursue a foreign policy as independent from the major powers at the beginning of the Cold War. Bazargan believed that Iran's policy towards the great powers should be similar to "Mossadegh's policy". This non-alignment policy, known more often as "the negative balance" policy, supposed to preserve Iran's independence by ending British domination Mosaddegh described this policy as following: "According to historical experiences, the Iranian nation is seriously interested in gaining independence and won't lose it at any cost. The nation wants foreigners to leave the country and not to interfere in our affairs, and expects that it will respect its independence in its meaning".[173] "The Iranian people want to have political balance,

---

[170] The Nixon Doctrine (also known as the Guam Doctrine) was put forth during a press conference in Guam on July 25, 1969 by US President Richard Nixon[1] and later formalized in his speech on Vietnamization on November 3, 1969. According to Gregg Brazinsky, Nixon stated that "the United States would assist in the defense and developments of allies and friends", but would not "undertake all the defense of the free nations of the world."

[171] The Alliance of the periphery or the Periphery doctrine is a foreign policy strategy that called for Israel to develop close strategic alliances with non-Arab Muslim states in the Middle East to counteract the united opposition of Arab states to the existence of Israel.

[172] Azghandi A. Foreign policy of the Islamic Republic of Iran // Tehran: Qumis, 2005.

[173] Ostovan H. Negative balance policy in the 14th Iranian majlis, Volume 1 // Tehran: Mossadegh, 1976.

that is, the balance in favor of this country and that is a negative balance. The Iranian nation will never agree on a positive balance". Bazargan also sought to end the dominant influence of the United States, just like Mossadegh, by breaking the Shah's unity with the United States. According to Karim Sanjabi, the first Minister of foreign affairs of Iran, Iran's policy of non-alignment was based on four pillars: "History, the geopolitical position of the country, the spiritual (moral) and human ideals of Islam, and the principle of full reciprocity in relations with other countries".[174]

In order to realize this policy, Iran expelled from the Central Treaty Organization (Cento) on March 3, 1979, joined the Non-Aligned Movement (NAM) and abolished many of the weapons-related purchases from the West. These orders included the purchase of $ 12 billion of warfare and 80 of the American fighter aircrafts F-14[175]. During completing this action, not only the U.S. intelligence bases were dismantled near the Soviet border in Iran, but also Ebrahim Yazdi, who served as minister of foreign affairs in the office instead of Sanjabi on April 12, 1979 called treaty defense summit between Iran and the USA (ratified on March 6, 1960) invalid. In the same time there was revocation of Articles 5 and 6 of the treaty of 1921 (27/02/1921) with the Soviet Union. Before it during the governance of Reza Shah Iran had tried several times to abolish the above mentioned articled, but had no success. The two articles were the same pretext that the Soviet Union considered it legitimate to force Iran to excuse its security.

Acceptance of the non-aligned movement strategy, which was strengthened by an independent stand of Iran, opened a new chapter in history and changed the direction of the "supporting state" of a "depending one". It was a term used by Gasiorowski M. J. to describe the state of foreign policy and the relations between Iran and the United States before the revolution[176].

The non-alignment strategy was the result of four major political goals of Tehran:

1.   Achieving independence in foreign decision-making;

2.   Refusal to intervene directly in the U.S.-Soviet competition;

3.   Ending the dependence on one ideological camp;

4.   Improving relations with all governments (except for Israel and the former South African regime)[177]

According to the Iranian foreign minister Sanjabi, these goals come from Iran's history, politics, geopolitics and religion. In the same time, foreign policy choices made by Shah and the historic needs of Iranians to gain independence in the field of foreign policy played an important

[174] Mahdavi A. H. Iranian foreign policy during the Pahlavi era of 1951-1978 // Tehran: Alborz, 1994.
[175] The Grumman F-14 Tomcat is an American supersonic, twin-engine, two-seat, variable-sweep wing fighter aircraft.
[176] Gasiorowski M. J. American foreign policy and the Shah, translated by Fereidoun Fatemi // Tehran: Center, 1992.
[177] 16.   Sadri Houman, Revolutionary states leader, foreign relations // New York: Praeger Press, 1997.

role in shaping Iran's foreign relations. As a result, the main goal of the foreign policy of the revolutionary time was to avoid all political, economic and cultural forms of both Western capitalism and East socialism.

Government of Mir Hossein Mousavi (1981-1989)

Value-centered or idealistic discourse

Another important discourse after the end of the period of realism in Iran's foreign policy is known as value-based discourse. The dominance of value-centered or idealistic discourse between the 1960s and 1970s and the decision-makers and implementers of foreign policy were all ideological, the ethical/mpral values were beyond the national interests, therefore, in the international context the reliance on this foreign policy approach is confronted on the international scene.[178] As a result of the goals pursued by Iranian foreign policy in recent years, they included the plan to export an Islamic Revolution, the statement of Jihad in two dimensions of cultural and military affairs, the theme of the arrogance and awakening of the oppressed nations, the awakening of the Muslim nations of the world, especially the awakening of the marginalized nations of the Persian Gulf. Following the policy of interfering in the affairs of others, firstly, actors in the field of international relations considered the Islamic Republic as an overwhelming force in the world order, and secondly, in the region, many countries considered Iran as a potential threatening national security issue. This negative aspect of foreign policy can be seen in relations between the Islamic Republic and international organizations, especially with the United Nations. Iran considered the organization as an instrument for legitimizing decisions of veto-based countries, and had some kind of political distrust towards the organization. This illegitimate and incorrect encounter with the organization in the Iran-Iraq war worsened this distrust, so that the Islamic Republic of Iran was trying not to commit to UN decisions. Among the features of this discourse are: 1. The authenticity of the Islamic Ummah. 2. The authenticity of the relations nation to nation. 3. Following the ideological goals. 4. The originality of Islamism in the development of the national identity. 5. Failure to accept the existing order and international order. 6. Non-commitment orientation means changing the status quo. 7. Supporting the right to determine the fate of nations. 8. Combating arrogance.[179]

The requirements for living in the interconnected international system have been reduced to realistic approaches to Iran's foreign policy. The Islamic system of Iran was able to identify its facilities and limitations to a large extent and to take steps to rebuild its relations with other

---

[178] Azghandi A. Op.cit.
[179] Firouzabadi S. J. D. Op.cit.

countries. The Islamic Republic has put economic reform into action in order to regulate the internal situation and rebuild the country. The central element of the ruling discourse in that period (pragmatic interest-oriented discourse), pragmatism in the formulation and implementation of foreign policy was the observance of Islamic values. In fact, the practical and behavioral policy of Iran in the field of foreign policy in the second decade of the revolution can be studied regarding national interests and regional arrangements and refrain from provoking others in the framework of the normalization of relations policy[180].

Starting from the year of 1361 (1982) after the ending of isolation, Imam Khomeini set the foreign policy of "Opening the doors" for Iran in Mordad 1362 (August 1983). According to Hujjat al-Islam (Hojatoleslam)[181] Khamenei's a policy is rational, justified and healthy relations with all countries which is aimed at serving Iran's interests and ideology. Imam himself on November 6, 1984, stated: "The lack of relations with other countries does not accept any wisdom and no human ... because it means its failure, destruction and even death..." This is the "new thinking" of Iran, which Hashemi Rafsanjani called "interdependence". In the field of foreign policy, the government of Mousavi, while bearing on foreign pressures, has tried to bring the world's public opinion with him, so that Iraq's invasion of Iran can be recognized. The most important thing in this period was the adoption of resolution 598 on Iran, which led to the end of military conflicts between the two countries.[182]

Mousavi was looking for a united Islamic front, but the first commander of the Islamic Revolutionary Guard Corps had criticized it. Government of Mir-Hossein Mousavi did not last for a long time but as most of the propaganda work was accomplished, there was a motive for him to obtain power as the prime minister. Also, most of the headlines of newspapers and magazines were covered with the speeches of his assignment and sentences about, for example, United Islamic Front, which was usually seen as a slogan and was occupying special part of the time when Mousavi was being a prime minister for 2-3 month. Mousavi is one of those people who can make good speeches and say that if we can work, we can manage the country well but when it comes to action, there is a

---

[180] Mozaffari M. ISLAMIST POLICY. Iranian Ideological Foreign Policy. Bin Laden's Foreign Policy. Paths of Amity and Enmity // Centre for Studies in Islamism and Radicalisation (CIR) Department of Political Science, Aarhus University, Denmark, 2009. [electronic source]. Available at: http://cir.au.dk/fileadmin/site_files/filer_statskundskab/subsites/cir/pdf-filer/Mozaffari_Papers.pdf (reference date: 09.09.2016).

[181] Hujjat al-Islam (from Arabic: ḥujjatu l-Islām) (also Hojatoleslam) is an honorific title meaning "authority on Islam" or "proof of Islam"

[182] Thirty-five-year anniversary of the Islamic Revolution. What did the eight Presidents have done for the progress of it? 2013. [electronic source]. Available at: http://www.khabaronline.ir/detail/337238/Politics/government (reference date: 09.09.2016).

big distance from slogan to action. After the fall of the Banisadr government and the elimination of liberals by the revolutionary forces, it is possible to consider the year of 1360 (1981) as the new phase of the Islamic Revolution.

After the association of Mohammad-Ali Rajai in a bombing, Sayyid Ali Hosseini Khamenei was elected to the presidency of the Islamic Republic of Iran. At the same stage Imam issued an order of preserving Islam and even primacy in relation to praying. The confirmation on rationality along with idealistic views became the obvious feature. The Iran-Iraq war that lasted eight years was the dominant crisis during this period, the unconsciousness of cultural, system economic and political system created a special case. In fact, attempts to conceal the class distance and maintain the integrity of the Islamic system were fundamental priorities. Iran's practical and behavioral policy in the field of foreign policy in the second decade of the revolution is seen regarding national interests and regional arrangements, avoiding incitement of others in the form of a policy of normalization of relations. [183]

In general, this foreign policy approach must be based on Islamic teachings and principles/standards and the realization of Islamic ideals and values. In these years, the decision-makers and policy makers were completely ideological. The value-based approach is established on traditional and abstract principles, moral values, and go far beyond the national interests. That is why, in the international environment, where the main actors' behavior is based on realism, reliance only on this foreign policy approach meets problems in the international scene. The practical weakness of this approach can be seen in the policy of contacting nations rather than governments. In other words, the idealistic approach in its radical form, while creating opportunities to meet transnational goals in the field of political influence, ideological unity, and the formation of a sphere of influence at the regional and international levels, also created limitations to national goals, industrial-technological development, economic prosperity and, in particular, international credibility.[184] Since the mid-1960s, which is the mid-war period of the Iran-Iraq war, the Ummah-based approach gradually became influenced by domestic problems and international pressure on a center-oriented approach with the emphasis on the need to defend the territorial integrity and preserve Shiite Umm al-Qur'a. In fact, during the eight years of the Iran-Iraq war, the ruling discourse was a lot influenced by the individual interests of leaders and ideology with a revisionist

[183] Kiasat H., Afshooni M. Iran's diplomatic behavior from the Revolution until the end of the war // Islamic Azad University, 2016. [electronic source]. Available at: http://docsdrive.com/pdfs/medwelljournals/sscience/2016/4224-4230.pdf (reference date: 01.05.2017).

[184] Darwisha A. Islam in foreign policy // Cambridge university press, 1983.

orientation in foreign relations; therefore, the fundamental concepts in the field of domestic politics and foreign relations were newly defined. According to this approach, not only institutionalization of idealistic ideology should be maintained in Iran and hegemonic place be held, but also there should be an attempt to define its scope through the establishment of multiple centers of resistance to global hegemony, beyond the geographic boundaries and challenge the global system. Minister of Foreign Affairs (1981-1997) Ali Akbar Velayati, who was one of the main supporters and actors of this discourse, says that the Islamic Republic not only is obliged to strive for the transformation of the foundations of the tyrannical powers and the outrageous global relations, but it should provide the real security in the shadow of this change. In short, the Islamic Republic of Iran, during the years of 1981-1989 attempted to undermine the rules and norms of foreign policy regardless of the international system, which replaced them. In this regard, the new foreign policy of Iran made its nations its audience, in the hope that it would be able to achieve the goals of the Islamic Revolution by connecting with them. The goals pursued by foreign policy in these years include: exporting of the Islamic Revolution, interpretation of the of jihad in two cultural and military dimensions, arrogance and awakening of the oppressed nations, awakening of the Muslim nations of the world, especially the those of the Gulf states due to its cultural and religious affiliations. Following the policy of interfering in the affairs of others, firstly, actors in the field of international relations made the Islamic Republic come off as a disruptive force in international order; the regional influence has also led many countries to consider Iran as a potential threat to national security. As a result, many countries, especially the Gulf States who were more vulnerable to other countries, were cautious in their relations with the Islamic Republic. This negative aspect of foreign policy can be seen in the Islamic Republic's relations with international organizations, and in particular with the United Nations[185]. The Islamic Republic of Iran was only in the process of being identified by other countries of the United Nations Organization. Based on a system of "Neither East nor West", the Islamic Republic evaluated its rights and interests, which were monopolized by the great powers. In addition, because this organization is considered as a means to legitimize the decisions of the countries disposing "power of veto", there was a kind of political distrust towards this organization. The irrational and incorrect treatment of this organization in the Iran-Iraq war has multiplied this distrust, and so the Islamic Republic was trying not to commit to UN decisions. Adoption of the United Nations Security Council Resolution 598 S/RES/0598 (1987), (UNSC resolution 598) and

---

[185] Impact on foreign policy // RAND
[electronic source]. Available at:
https://www.rand.org/content/dam/rand/pubs/monograph_reports/MR1320/MR1320.ch6.pdf   (reference   date:
01.05.2016).

the formation of a cease-fire in the Iran-Iraq war can be seen as a milestone in the political developments in Iran. On July 18, 1988 Hashemi Rafsanjani stated that the adoption of the resolution and its aftermath would form a new chapter in Iran's political history. At this stage, the most obvious signs of change in Iran are foreign policy issues. Hashemi said: "The most important issue is that due to the adoption of the resolution and the cease-fire we can stop the process of hostility that has been created. This action has brought us a new path. Recently, individuals and countries have provided effective facilities to Saddam Hussein. If they were not worried about us, they would not do that." Due to this change, we see the transformations in the direction of Iran's foreign policy. In the new period, revolutionary idealism replaced realism.[186]

After the death of the Supreme Leader of the Revolution and the revision of the constitution, the members of the Supreme National Security Council headed Hashemi Rafsanjani, who was recently President of Iran, had a consensus that the Islamic Republic could not survive without the expansion of the Islamic revolution outside its borders. Therefore, foreign policy decision makers assumed the Islamic Republic of Iran as "the mother of Islamic lands", which could be the center and base for Islamic fundamentalist movements. According to them, Islamic fundamentalist movements would not be able to achieve power in their countries without the material and spiritual/moral support of the Islamic Republic, while the activities of these fundamentalist movements could only isolate the Islamic Republic. Throughout the years of the war, Iran's security frontiers were located far beyond the official borders of the country. Slogans such as "Freedom to Karbala and al-Quds (Jerusalem) and "Destruction of Israel" were regarded as the main policy in the foreign policy of the Islamic Republic. On the other hand, during the first ten years of the republic, internal interactions in Iran were accompanied by the rise of radicalism in the Middle East region, as well as the intensification of Islamist waves and the return to Islamic principles and history in some of the countries of the region. In a way that the Islamic Republic of Iran was the main source of leading (guiding), Islamic fundamentalism was replaced. In fact, the policy of exporting the revolution at this time has added the concern to the moderate and conservative countries of the region that came from the emergence of revolutionary movements similar to those of Iran in their own countries. This unequal structure, economic problems, military obstacles in the end led Iranian politicians to provide a theoretical line based on the priority of "Islam in one country" rather than the theory of export of revolution. The end of Iran-Iraq war and adoption of the resolution 598 in fact

---

[186] Sadeghi B., Tabatabai S. M. Metaphor Analysis and Discursive Cycle of Iran's Foreign Policy: "Justice" through the lenses of US-IRAN Presidents // Cumhuriyet University Faculty of Science Science Journal, 2015. [electronic source]. Available at: http://dergi.cumhuriyet.edu.tr/cumuscij/article/viewFile/5000121835/5000114490 (reference date: 01.05.2016).

were based on this new point of view that took precedence of Al-Qura theory over the interests of the Islamic world. From the point of view of Larijani Islamic Republic of Iran follows 3 vital goals: 1) Maintaining the Islamic nature of the regime and its position in the Islamic world; 2) Protection and defense of the country's security; 3) Development of the Islamic Republic of Iran. In fact, according to the doctrine of Al-Qura if a country among Islamic countries, it becomes Al-Qura daralaslam. In such a way that failure or victory of that country is considered to be failure or victory of the whole Islamic world. In this case the priority is saving the Al-Qura.[187] In addition to the dialectical relations between Al-Qura and the Islamic world as an important component of the Al-Qura doctrine, it also has other essential components. Indeed, a country can be Al-Qura of the Islamic world if it has a charismatic leadership and deserves the full leadership of the Islamic Ummah. Therefore, disposing of strategic location, population, ancestry and etc. cannot be the point of issue, while the criteria of "velayat"[188] can. After the victory of Islamic revolution in Iran and Imam's guidance Iran became Al-Qura daralaslam and it was his duty to take the lead of the Islamic world. As the Ummah, it was its duty to choose "velayat", which means Iran's leadership in the whole Ummah[189].

In conclusion, it can be noted that during the post-revolutionary period until the very end of the Iran-Iraq war Iran has experienced two discourses, which had few differences. Thus, the first discourse was called realistic, the main characteristics of which were, first of all, non-alignment and it is in this period of time that the very famous slogan of "Neither East nor West" appeared. In fact it was a reflection of the existing world order and Iran's will not to make part of a sphere of a struggle between the big powers (the USSR and Great Britain, for example, as it was in the past). In the same time Iran was only denying the domination itself, and did not have a purpose of disruption relations with other countries. The second discourse was highly influenced by the Iran-Iraq war and adoption of the resolution on cease-fire, when Iran was morally and physically tired of a long-lasting conflict. Also, Iran did not want to be isolated, while export of the Islamic Revolution was seen by many countries (first of all those of the Persian Gulf) as the potential threat.

---

[187] Bastani H. How Powerful is Rouhani in the Islamic Republic? // Middle East and North Africa Programme, 2004. [electronic source]. Available at: https://www.chathamhouse.org/sites/files/chathamhouse/field/field_document/20141124RouhaniislamicRepublicBastani.pdf (reference date: 01.02.2017).

[188] The Guardianship of the Islamic Jurist, also called the Governance of the Jurist (Persian : Vilayat-e Faqih; Arabic: Wilayat al-Faqih), is a post-Age-of-Occultation theory in Shia Islam which holds that Islam gives a faqīh (Islamic jurist) custodianship over people. Ulama supporting the theory disagree over how encompassing custodianship should be.

[189] Veldani A. J. Iran and international law // Tehran: pazineh publications, 2001.

2.3. Relations of Iran and Syria, Iran and Saudi Arabia during the eight-year Iran-Iraq war

The role of Syria in the eight-year war

The outbreak of the war between the two countries represents threats and in the same time gives possibilities for the third countries, which take a certain stand. The Iran-Iraq war was no exception to this rule. Just in the beginning of the war, the third countries defined their position in accordance with the notion of national interests, threats and opportunities. In this context, the position of the Arab countries was very important given that Iraq was an Arab country. Except for Syria and Libya, other Arab countries either supported Iraq or took neutral stance. During this war, Syria's position as one of the most important countries of the Middle East, and at the same time, borders with Iraq, had significant implications. While Syria, as a member of the Arab League, was expected to assist Iraq in its war against a non-Arab state, it adopted a strategic policy as Iran's most important alliance, and its relations in the military and economy field only enhanced its ties with Iran. Syria's strategy, due to the close ties with the Soviet Union and the Eastern bloc, contributed to the complexity of the analysis of the Iran-Iraq war in international relations and the attitude of the two superpowers, which led the Iran-Iraq war to the ethnic splits of Persians and Arabs or Shiites and Sunnis. [190]

Review of relations between Syria and Iran

The ups-and-downs of relations between these two countries during the Pahlavi government were quite remarkable. During this period, these relations were influenced by relations between Iran and Israel and were also within the framework of defending the interests of the Arab world. Although the two countries had diplomatic and economic ties with each other, the level of these relations was by no means desirable. The fall of the Shah and the victory of the Islamic Revolution led to the widespread and strategic cooperation between the two countries, and the revolution created the emergence of a new regional order. The true power of revolutionary Islam proved that the possibility of building a new, Iran-centered regional order is not necessarily an idea. The new

---

[190] Smith W. Our Defense is a Holy Defense! - The Iran-Iraq War and its Legacy in Contemporary Iranian Factional Politics // Journal of Georgetown University-Qatar. Middle Eastern Studies Students Association, 2015. [electronic source]. Available at: http://www.qscience.com/doi/pdf/10.5339/messa.2015.3 (reference date: 01.02.2016).

government of Tehran quickly established strong ties with Syria and the Palestine Liberation Organization (PLO). In this regard, the anti-Israeli tendency of this government was the basis of this alliance.[191]

Although the Islamic Revolution of Iran, contrary to Ba'ath thought, was a factor of awakening Islamic forces, the Syrian government, under the leadership of Hafez al-Assad, supported this revolution, and Syria was among the first Arab states to recognize Iran's new political regime. Also, because of the Alawites branch of Islam, Syrian leader was always welcoming the revolutionary Shiite wave.[192] Iran's anti-Israeli position and the support given to the Palestinian struggle against Israel have made Syria's positive attitude towards Iran. The Islamic revolution created a fundamental transformation in Iranian governance structures, especially in the field of foreign policy. Thus, after the revolution, Iran's foreign policy strategy was based on the principle of Neither East nor West, rejection of any domination and oppression, support for revolutionary movements in Islamic countries, and the attempt to export the Islamic Revolution to other Islamic countries.[193] This possibility of revolutionary ideas in the countries of the region in terms of the existence of dissident groups in these countries was the reason why most of Iran's neighbors, especially the Arab countries, have seen the Islamic revolution as a threat to their security.[194]

This view led the Islamic Republic of Iran to be under the diplomatic pressure, so that at the same time as the beginning of the military invasion of Iran, Iran was in isolation from the point of view of foreign policy. Due to the fact that the Islamic Revolution changed regional and international balance, the Iraqi military invasion in Iran provided the implicit of the two superpowers (the USA and the USSR), as well as of many of the conservative countries of the region. In such a situation, strategy of Iran's foreign policy was to attract the friendly countries and get a support during the war. In fact, the positive stance of countries of such as Syria, Libya, South Yemen and the Palestine Liberation Organization, all of which were considered as Arab countries, was important for Iran, so it tried saving and maintaining this support. In this regard, Syrian support was more important among the countries mentioned, because: 1) For Iran, Syria was one of the most important countries Middle East region with a high influence among other countries; 2) Syrian support for Iran, having widespread land borders and severe disagreements with Iraq, made Iraq always feel unsecure from the side of Syria; the unity of Iran and Syria could have reduced greater expansionism of Iraq; 3) Due to the experience of wars with Israel, Syria was considered as one of

---

[191] Hussein J. Agha and Ahmad. Syria and Iran (rivalry and cooperation) // London Wellington House, 1995.
[192] Seale Op.cit.
[193] Constitution of the Islamic Republic of Iran // Tehran: Publishing House Jihad University, 1991.
[194] Hussein J.Agha and Ahmad, Op.cit.

the powerful countries of the region in terms of military skills and weapons, and could have helped Iran if it was necessary. On the other hand, in the international level, there were close relations between Syria and the Soviet Union and it was an important channel for Iran, as this superpower was close to the northern border of Iran.[195] Despite the repression of the supporters of the Soviet Union and Tudeh Party of Iran[196] by the revolutionary forces, Iranian authorities knew that they needed to maintain relations with the USSR. Although relations between the two countries were always established, their level was quite law due to the possible danger for the Muslim republics of the Soviet Union coming from ideas of export of revolutionary ideas. Meanwhile, the positive role of Syria could have contributed to a positive Soviet position to respond to Iran's arsenal needs during the war. In fact, Iran's prediction took place and Syria became an important channel for transferring Russian weapons to Iran.[197] For Syria, relations with Iran also were important. The Iranian Revolution caused Syria to escape from the many problems that it faced with the previous regime in Iran, and instead of a government that was in conflict with the interests of Syria, the new government that had come to power, had a lot of interests with the Damascus government. Even though the Iran-Iraq war was opposed to the Syrian leaders, somehow it switched Iraq's attention from Syria to the other.

For Syria, the Iraq's invasion to Iran revealed an outbreak of military defeat and the fall of Saddam's regime. At most, a prolonged and heavy war for Iraq in Iran's land, destroyed potential was the ideal for the Damascus government and, on a large scale, had the opportunity for Hafez al-Assad's government to maneuver in the East. In addition, the Iran-Iraq war led Syria to pursue active diplomacy at the regional level and since Syria was highly skilled in this field, achieve significant political and economic benefits through diplomatic methods.

Actions took by Syria in the Iran-Iraq war

Syria's actions during the Iran-Iraq war can be divided into three specific periods. The first phase, starts from the beginning of the military invasion of Iraq to Iran and its progress on the territory of this country until facing the popular resistance and stop of the progress of the Iraqi forces. The second phase starts from the beginning of the successful military operations of Iran until the liberation of Khorramshahr and the retreat of Iraqi forces behind the international borders. The

---

[195] Ibid.
[196] The Tudeh Party of Iran (Persian: Ḥezb-e Tūde-ye Īrān, lit. 'Party of the Masses of Iran') is an Iranian communist party. Formed in 1941, with Soleiman Mohsen Eskandari as its head, it had considerable influence in its early years and played an important role during Mohammad Mosaddegh's campaign to nationalize the Anglo-Persian Oil Company and his term as prime minister.
[197] Ibid.

third phase lasts since the beginning of successful operations pf Iran on the territory of Iraq and the occupation of some parts of Iraq, implementing the punishment strategy for the aggressor until the adoption of United Nations Security Council resolution 598 S/RES/0598 (1987). During each of these phases, Syria's strategy of support was to protect Iran from severity and weakness, and it was shaped by conditions that were militarily and politically motivated.

The first phase (from the beginning of the invasion of Iraq to the splintering of its forces)

The Iraqi invasion of Iran on September 22, 1980 helped create the necessary ground for a predictable alliance between Syria and Iran. Based on reports, Hafez al-Assad refused to accept the request of the Special Envoy pf the Islamic republic of Iran to release a statement in support of the country on September 25, 1980. Certainly, the Syrian authorities worried that Iraq would achieve a decisive and rapid victory against Iran; therefore, under the critical conditions of the first days of the war, the protection of Iran, which they believed could have failed, was a huge risk. Nevertheless, Syria sent to Iran some weapons and equipment, including surface-to-air missile (SAM), anti-tank missiles of Russia and artillery ammunition[198].

With the suspension of the progress of the Iraq's army and the failure of the country's military attempt to defeat Iran, Syria decided to take a firm stand in condemning Iraq and supporting Iran. In this regard, Syria, accusing Iraq of the agent of imperialism, blamed the war for the benefit of the United States and for the Arabs to deflect against Israel, it also criticized Iraq for having opted instead for dealing with Iran and exploiting its potential to confront Israel in its invasion[199].

At this stage, Syria's support for Iran was taking place in two phases: political and military. In the political arena, Hafez al-Assad, was trying to convince the kings of Saudi Arabia and Jordan to put pressure on Saddam to stop the war. Also, during an official visit to the Soviet Union soon after the beginning of the war, he issued a joint declaration with Brezhnev to support Iran's inalienable right to an independent fate without any foreign influence[200]. One of Syria's most important actions during this period was avoiding the formation of a united Arab front against Iran. The country questioned the nationalist tendencies and Iraqi policies in the Arab world, despite the large amount of propaganda showing the war between Iran and Iraq, as a war between the Arabs and Persians, and the continued wars under the name of Islam. However, Iraq succeeded in attracting

---

[198] Byman D. Strange Bedfellows. What's behind the enduring alliance between Syria and Iran?, 2006. [electronic source]. Available at: http://www.slate.com/articles/news_and_politics/foreigners/2006/07/strange_bedfellows.html (reference date: 03.05.2016).
[199] Seale. Op. cit.
[200] Chapter V. Syria and Her Non-Arab Neighbours [electronic source]. Available at: http://shodhganga.inflibnet.ac.in/bitstream/10603/17356/10/10_chapter%205.pdf (reference date: 11.04.2016).

financial and military support to many Arab countries. At the Arab summit in Amman in 1980, Syrian opposition did not let formation of the Arab bloc to support Iraq to occur[201].

The second phase (from the Operation Samen-ol-A'emeh to the Liberation of Khorramshahr)

During this period, Iran was able to take the initiative in the war. The popularization of the war, the purification of Iran's political structure from the non-revolutionary and liberal forces and the coherence created by the military structure, including strengthening of the Islamic Revolutionary Guard Corps[202] as a revolutionary force, led to the mobilization of the collective will of the country; a process that was the outcome of a successful military operation. Due to the Operation Samen-ol-A'emeh[203], the Operation Fath ol-Mobin[204] and Jerusalem[205] a large part of the occupied territories were recaptured, and Iraqi forces were pushed behind the international borders. Iran's military successes made Syria to follow a strategy that was adopted in the wake of the war. Following these victories, Syria could easily open up its position in support of Iran. During this period, relations between Iran and Syria expanded in all areas. Syria has begun extensive consultations and its political efforts to put pressure on Iraq and change the conference place of Non-aligned movement from Baghdad to another country. These efforts, with Iran's military actions to insecure Baghdad for such a conference, eventually led to the transfer of the conference place from Baghdad to New Delhi, and, in this regard, seriously damaged the international reputation of Iraq[206].

The third phase (from the beginning of the aggressive punishment policy to the end of the war)

With the success of the Iranian military forces in rejecting the Iraq's army behind the international borders and liberating the occupied territories, taking into account the personality of Saddam Hussein at the head of the Iraqi government, in the political and military authorities of Iran, there was an idea that there was no peaceful resolution to end the war between the two countries.

---

[201] Ibid.

[202] The Islamic Revolutionary Guard Corps (IRGC) (in Persian: Sepāh-e Pāsdārān-e Enqelāb-e Eslāmi, lit. 'Army of the Guardians of the Islamic Revolution' or Sepāh for short) is a branch of Iran's Armed Forces founded after 1979 Revolution.

[203] Operation Samen-ol-A'emeh (Persian: "Operation Eighth Imam") was an offensive of the Iran-Iraq war between 27–29 September 1981 where Iran broke the Iraqi Siege of Abadan.

[204] Operation Fath ol-Mobin (Persian: Quranic phrase meaning "Undeniable Victory" or "Manifest Victory") was a major Iranian military operation conducted during the Iran-Iraq War, in March 1982.

[205] Operation Beit-ol-Moqaddas (Jerusalem) was an Iranian operation conducted during the Iran–Iraq War. The operation was a success, in as so far as it achieved its standing aim of liberation of Khorramshahr and pushing Iraqi troops back to the border. This operation, coupled with Operation Tariq al-Qods, and Operation Undeniable Victory, succeeded in evicting Iraqi troops from southern Iran and gave Iran the momentum.

[206] Lotfollahzadegan A. The Iran-Iraq War, Crossing the Border // Tehran: Center for War Studies and Research, 2002.

Under the influence of this idea, they refused to accept any mediation and resolution from third countries for peace, and they imposed a strategy of punishing the aggressor and overthrowing the Iraqi regime. In this regard, extensive and successful operations were carried out, including such operations as the Operation Kheibar[207], the Operation Dawn 8[208], the Siege of Basra (Operation Karbala-5)[209], the Operation Dawn 10, the result of which was that strategic areas, as, for example, Majnoon Island, Bandar Al-Faw, areas of eastern Basra and Northern Iraq were captured by the Iranian forces, and the Iraqi army suffered irreparable damage, its strength was severely depleted, and the south front was on the brink of collapse. In this period, of war, Iraq's defeat and the possible victory of Iran showed the will of the world powers and the countries of the region to prevent Iran's military victory and strengthen the military power of Iraq. Thus, the United States and the Soviet Union provided Iraq with a lot of economic, military and intelligence assistance.[210] Their goal was to create a balance of power between the two countries and exert pressure on Iran and Iraq to end the war. This issue was necessary, especially after the geographic area of the war expanded to the Persian Gulf, and it threatened the flow of oil exports from the region.

The relations between Syria and the Islamic Republic of Iran during the eight-year war are seen as an objective symbol the policy-making based on national interests. These relations, formed in the framework of the interests and needs of the two countries, are divided into three periods of time that at each stage, the level of cooperation and relationship between the two countries has direct relations with the needs and developments of the region and the world. In the first phase, Syria was pleased with the fact that the Iran-Iraq war had involved Saddam's regime, and in order to increase the confidence of the resistance of the Iranian army against the invasion of Iraq, it took the side of Tehran; a situation in which Iran gained significant political and military opportunities. During the second phase, Syria gained prominence from its alliance with Iran and the Economic Protocol between the two countries providing export of cheap oil to Syria was signed. During the third phase, the military situation of the battle fronts and the widespread military success of Iran and the formation of a single regional and global policy to end the war without a winner and loser put Syrian positions in support of Iran under pressure. At this point, the Syrian government had to choose

---

[207] Operation Kheibar was an Iranian offensive in the Iran–Iraq War. It was part of the Battle of the Marshes.

[208] Operation Dawn 8 was an Iranian military operation conducted during the Iran–Iraq War, part of the First Battle of al-Faw.

[209] The Siege of Basra, code-named Operation Karbala-5 , was an offensive operation carried out by Iran in an effort to capture the Iraqi port city of Basra in early 1987. This battle, known for its extensive casualties and ferocious conditions, was the biggest battle of the war and proved to be the beginning of the end of the Iran–Iraq War.

[210] Why did the U.S. support Saddam in the Iran-Iraq War, but fought against him in Kuwait? // Quora, 2016. [electronic source]. Available at: https://www.quora.com/Why-did-the-US-support-Saddam-in-the-Iran-Iraq-War-but-fought-against-him-in-Kuwait (reference date: 11.02.2017).

between the benefits and losses of cooperation with Iran. In a complex diplomacy, while maintaining friendly relations with Iran, Syria responded positively to mediation plans of the conservative Arab countries to solve problems with Iraq. Despite the initial advances in resolving the disputes between Syria and Iraq, due to the fact that the above-mentioned disputes turned to the nature of the government of the two countries, little progress was made, and improving relations between them is unlikely to happen. During this process, the Syrian government came to the conclusion that its interests would be better served in partnership with Iran, and therefore, continued its support of Iran on the diplomacy agenda. On the other hand, Iran also became more aware of the importance of having an ally like Syria, and with the efforts of both sides they resolved the problems that existed in the development of relations between the two countries. In order to show its goodwill, the Islamic Republic of Iran, while guaranteeing the export of cheap oil to Syria, also coordinated more with the Syrian strategy in Lebanon, and Syria continued to maintain its support of Iran until the end of the war. Adoption of the United Nations Security Council Resolution 598 and the end of the eight-year war created the basis for broader cooperation between the two countries at the regional and international levels. After the war, relations between Iran and Syria were affected by regional and global developments. The collapse of the Soviet Union influenced foreign policy of Syria, which strongly relied on its support. In this period, Syria was severely damaged by Israel due to loss of Soviet support. Also, with the tensions that Syria had with Turkey in supporting the Kurds, there was a threat by his northern neighbor.[211] On the other hand, Iraq has become a potential security threat to Syria due to the high military capability that it had accumulated during the war with Iran. In this regard, Syria strongly needed the continuation of its engagement with Iran. However, after the war, the two countries did not have relations within the framework of the wartime relationship, but the two countries tried to implement a single strategy in the region, a matter that was shown in the positions against the Iraq's invasion of Kuwait and the U.S. war with this country in 1991.

The role of Saudi Arabia in the eight-year war between Iran and Iraq

The beginning of the Iraq's invasion in Iran on September 22, 1980 gave Saudi Arabia an opportunity to act alongside Saddam Hussein against the new regime of the Islamic Republic of Iran.[212] During the eight years of the Imposed by the Ba'athist regime war against Iran, Saudi Arabia did not hesitate to provide any political, financial, intelligence and arms support to Saddam; during

---

[211] Rodriquez C. The Iraqi Disarmament Crisis: What Lessons Can Be Learned? // E-International relations student, 2017. [electronic source]. Available at: http://www.e-ir.info/2017/10/02/the-iraqi-disarmament-crisis-what-lessons-can-be-learned/ (reference date: 02.11.2017)
[212] Katzman K. Opt.cit.

the Iraqi invasion of Kuwait (the Gulf war), Fahd of Saudi Arabia said: "The actions of the Iraqi leader (in invading Kuwait) indicate that military aid of Saudi Arabia has been ungrateful to him during his eight-year war against Iran; if Iraq says it has sacrificed its people, we have also contributed to this sacrifice with our money, our advanced weapons and our international cooperation. How can he forget all of this and try to eliminate the facts?"[213]. Al-Saud political authorities during the imposed war brought all their diplomatic capacities to isolate Iran and strengthen the Ba'ath regime in Iraq. Political consultations with various countries, including America, Egypt, Jordan, Morocco, etc. were among the measures taken in this regard. Another action made by the Saudi regime was to dominate the Organization of the Islamic Conference and to change its constitution and its laws in order to exert pressure on Iran. In addition, one of the most influential channels also was the Gulf Cooperation Council, which was governed by the Saudis themselves. On one hand, Al Saud reinforced the military and political aspects of this council; on the other, he was trying to undermine Iran by exerting pressure on Syria as the only Arab supporter of the Islamic Revolution in the Iran-Iraq war.[214]. In addition, after the conquest by the Islamic warriors in the Operation Dawn 8, the Cooperation Council for the Arab States of the Gulf had a meeting on March 4, 1985 where Iran was opposed. The biggest treason of Al Saud was cooperation with the Mujahedin Organization[215] in 1987 Mecca incident[216], which resulted in the rupture of relations between Tehran and Riyadh. Based on what Massoud Rajavi said in his hidden talks with the head of the Iraqi intelligence service, Saber Abdel Aziz al-Douri, the head of the group of Mujahedin, along with the events of Mecca, got an official invitation from Fahd bin Abdulaziz Al Saud and secretly traveled to Saudi Arabia in 1987.[217] In addition, in an interview with Dubai daily newspaper, the secretary general of the Gulf Cooperation Council, Hashem Al Maskari officially declared: "What happened in Mecca is not the consequence of the Iran-Iraq war". The Al Saud regime not only not succeed in doing so, but also at that time launched an oil war with the aim of

---

[213] Invasion Revisited: How Saudi Arabia backed Saddam's war on Iran? // The Iran Project, 2016. [electronic source]. Available at: http://theiranproject.com/blog/2016/09/28/invasion-revisited-saudi-arabia-backed-saddams-war-iran/ (reference date: 11.02.2017).

[214] The Imposed war and Oil - second part: the role of oil in the continuation of the Holy Defense // The site of the holy defense science and education research center [electronic source]. Available at: http://www.dsrc.ir/View/article.aspx?id=713 (reference date: 01.05.2016).

[215] The People's Mojahedin Organization of Iran or the Mojahedin-e Khalq (Persian: Sāzmān-e mojāhedin-e khalq-e irān, abbreviated MEK, PMOI or MKO) is an Iranian political–militant organization in exile that advocates the violent overthrow of the current regime in Iran, while claiming itself as the replacing government in exile.

[216] The 1987 Mecca incident was a clash between Shia pilgrim demonstrators and the Saudi Arabian security forces, during the Hajj pilgrimage; it occurred in Mecca on 31 July 1987 and led to the deaths of over 400 peop

[217] Kofner J. 400 die as Iranian marchers battle Saudi police in Mecca; embassies smashed in Teheran // The New York Times, 1987. [electronic source]. Available at: http://www.nytimes.com/1987/08/02/world/400-die-iranian-marchers-battle-saudi-police-mecca-embassies-smashed-teheran.html?pagewanted=all (reference date: 01.05.2016).

reducing the economic power and currency earnings of the Islamic Republic of Iran. By reducing oil prices, the Saudis tried to paralyze the Iranian economy. This reduction went up to $6 per barrel. Saudi Arabia, along with other oil producing countries, has been disrupting the production and export of Iranian oil by increasing production and saturation of the oil market. The Saudi actions, which were justified by "Market Share Strategy", aimed to keep oil prices low for one or two years[218].

For this reason, the Minister of Petroleum of Iran emphasized Al Saud's hostility at the 70th OPEC Summit: "The price war is an American action, which has begun in Saudi Arabia; the arrogant world by reducing oil prices and the Iranian economy intends to put the war under pressure". The fear of exposing Saudi Arabia's role in supporting Iraq has led the Saudis to hidden financial support of the opposition to the Islamic Republic. The oil dollars of Al Saud were the main source of Iraqi Ba'ath regime funding in the war. In 1982, shortly after the liberation of Khorramshahr[219] and the defeat of Ba'ath, it was known that Saddam received $20 billion from the Saudi regime and other Persian Gulf regimes to continue the war against the Islamic Revolution of Iran. The Iraqi regime was also provided $29 billion during the Operation Badr the Operation Dawn 8 by Saudi Arabia and Emirates[220].

In addition to this, Saudi governors played the role of financial mediation for Saddam in different arm contracts, when Saudi Arabia announced its readiness to pay for the weapons purchased from France by Iraq estimated over 10 billion francs during the war. On December 25, the Reuters news agency reported that Saudi Arabia's financial assistance of military and economic aid to Iraq was about $ 27 billion by the Saudi king. Fahd of Saudi Arabia said: "The total value of credits, loans and other types of aid that has been delivered to Iraq in the form of oil shipments or equipment was more than $ 27.5 billion. These items include $ 5.84 billion in credits, $ 6.75 billion in oil production, $ 9.25 billion in non-interest loans and $ 2.74 billion in military equipment and transportation". Financial aid of Al Saud reached up to the point that Iraq included all from the main military equipment to the most basic equipment needs of the Iraqi soldiers; all were provided with Saudi dollars[221]. After the Iraqi invasion in Kuwait, the Saudi defense minister said: "Iraq, which

[218] The 1979 "Oil Shock:" Legacy, Lessons, and Lasting Reverberations // The Middle East Institute, Washington, DC. [electronic source]. Available at: http://www.la.utexas.edu/users/chenry/public_html/elephants/OilShock201979-Final.pdf (reference date: 05.02.2016).

[219] The Liberation of Khorramshahr (Persian: Āzādsāzi-ye Khorramshahr) was the Iranian recapture of the port city of Khorramshahr from the Iraqis on 24 May 1982 during the Iran–Iraq War.

[220] Tabaar M. A. Factional politics in the Iran–Iraq war // Taylor & Francis, 2017. [electronic source]. Available at: http://www.tandfonline.com/doi/abs/10.1080/01402390.2017.1347873?tokenDomain=eprints&tokenAccess=r89yv6kfu 9MFqF8BqMtB&forwardService=showFullText&doi=10.1080%2F01402390.2017.1347873&doi=10.1080%2F014023 90.2017.1347873&journalCode=fjss20 (reference date: 05.02.2016).

[221] Invasion Revisited: How Saudi Arabia Backed Saddam's War on Iran? //Alwaght, 2016. [electronic source]. Available at: http://alwaght.com/en/News/68927/Invasion-Revisited-How-Saudi-Arabia-Backed-Saddam%E2%80%99s-War-on-Iran? (reference date: 01.03.2017).

today intends to threaten Saudi Arabia has perhaps forgotten that during the war with Iran even drinks for his soldiers were provided by us"[222]. In fact, the intelligence cooperation of the Al-Saud regime with Iraqi Ba'ath has been unprecedented in the history of the wars of a century. This intelligence cooperation shows that the Saudis sought to strike the Islamic Revolution of Iran by the victory of the Islamic Movement in September 22, 1980. Just a month and a half before the beginning of the war, Saudi government officials gave Saddam a gift, reports from the U.S. intelligence, in which economic, social and military conditions of Iran were described. In addition, during the imposed war, the Saudi regime, using the most advanced intelligence tools, including an airborne early warning and control (AEW&C) system, repeatedly provided some of the information collected by the United States to Iraq. It was important and strategic information that led to the dismantling of Iran's operations against Iraq, providing accurate satellite images of the position of the Iranian warriors and the manner in which the forces were arranged. In May 1984, Saddam Hussein confirmed receiving of such information[223].

On the other hand, Bandar bin Sultan Al Saud, Saudi Arabia's ambassador to the United States, said: "The Al Saud regime played a mediating role between Washington and Baghdad in the final years of the Iraq war; valuable military intelligence about Iran's movements to the battlefields was transmitted from US intelligence sources to the Baghdad regime. The Iraqis demanded most of all the U.S. military assistance to Iraq in the field of information and plans and military advisers against Iran, and Saudi Arabia provided all these facilities and even more".[224] The 39th President of the United States, Jimmy Carter referring to the fear of Saudi rulers of Iranian military power in this regard, said: "I spoke with the Saudi officials about the Iranian special threat and in order to ensure safety I decided to send some of the airborne early warning and control (AEW&C) system[225] to the peninsula. Also, I was prepared to send American F-15 to the United States to counter the Iranian F-4s". AEW&C aircrafts, advanced F-15 for launching bombs, airborne tankers for warhead bomber; space launchers and larger fuel tankers to expand the F-15s were part of the military equipment that the United States provided to Al Saud during the war against Iran[226].

---

[222] Mofid K. The cost of the Iran-Iraq war has been estimated at $1.097 billion // The Economic Consequences of the Gulf War. New York: Routlefge, 1990.

[223] Ibid.

[224] Holland J. The First Iraq War Was Also Sold to the Public Based on a Pack of Lies // Moyers & company, 2014. [electronic source]. Available at: http://billmoyers.com/2014/06/27/the-first-iraq-war-was-also-sold-to-the-public-based-on-a-pack-of-lies/ (reference date: 24.04.2016).

[225] An airborne early warning and control (AEW&C) system is an airborne radar picket system designed to detect aircraft, ships and vehicles at long ranges and perform command and control of the battlespace in an air engagement by directing fighter and attack aircraft strikes.

[226] Iran, the United States and a Political Seesaw // The New York Times, 2012. [electronic source]. Available at: http://www.nytimes.com/interactive/2012/04/07/world/middleeast/iran-timeline.html (reference date: 01.05.2016).

The Saudi arms support during the war was not providing weapons of mass destruction only, but it was also infrastructure in Iraq, where the transfer of military equipment from the port of Daman of Saudi Arabia took place. In addition, the Saudi regime was involved in direct military strikes. However, Fahd of Saudi Arabia admitted the Saudi role in equipping and increasing Iraq's power. Saudi and Saddam regimes have come to a close deal with the expansion of military cooperation against Iran. The Saudi regime has delivered a huge number of weapons to the Iraqi regime over the past 10 days, and there are other donations that are being given to save Saddam from the danger of a fall. The recent visit of Amir Abdollah to Baghdad had the same purpose. [227]

Paying attention to the supporting role of the Al Saud during of the imposed war reveals the depth of their hostility to the Islamic Revolution of Iran. At a press conference on 13/11/1369 (February 2, 1991), Fahd of Saudi Arabia while acknowledging his full support for the Ba'ath regime, expressed his hope that the Islamic Republic of Iran has forgotten all the tragic events that had taken place in the past between the Islamic Republic of Iran and the Gulf states.

Conclusion of the second chapter

In this chapter the characteristics of Iran's foreign policy in the Middle East under the leadership of Imam Khomeini are represented. The first part of the chapter explains the issue of islamization of the foreign policy of Iran, and it can be concluded that Imam Khomeini has a special place in understanding the principles and basics of foreign policy. What is worth mentioning is that Islam turned into a paradigm in foreign policy. The main points here are: independence, the export of revolution, the unity of the Islamic Ummah, respect for mutual rights, the negation of oppression, establishing good and peaceful relations with others, the defense of Islam and Muslims, the policy of the Neither East nor West and assistance to the liberation movements. The second part of this chapter explains the priorities of Iran's foreign policy in the Middle East region during the Bazargan and Mousavi government and it can be concluded that the Bazargan's government pursues a pragmatic and realistic discourse, while Mousavi's government the value-centered one. In the third part there is an analysis of the relations of Iran with Syria and Saudi Arabia during the 8-year war with Iraq (The Iran-Iraq war). It can be concluded that Saudi Arabia provided a lot of financial and logistical support to Iraq in order to defeat Iran, while Syria supported Iran. Syrian government considered that its interests would be better served in cooperation with it.

---

[227] Ibid.

Chapter 3. Fundamental features of Iran's foreign policy during the leadership of Imam Khamenei (1989-nowadays)

3.1. Priorities and Features of Iran's Foreign Policy in the governments of Rafsanjani, Khatami, Ahmadinejad and Rouhani

Adoption of the Security Council Resolution 598 and the end of Iran-Iraq war, revision of the constitution, election of Akbar Hashemi Rafsanjani to the presidency on the one hand, and collapse of the Soviet Union, its influence on international relations on the other hand were among the factors, that influenced the process of public policy system, way of thinking, decision making, the elites on both domestic and international levels. The ravages wrought by war, financial and moral problems resulting from it, the issue of immigrants and war veterans, the destruction of production centers, the reduction of national capital, the economic blockade as well as the economic turmoil and the obstacles of domestic politics seriously threatened the existence of the Islamic Republic. While providing policy of disregard for international agreements during the eight years of the war, none of the demands of international revisionism were provided. Under the influence of these factors and realities of the international system and internal and critical conditions, government was forced to accept it. In order to organize the internal situation and rebuild the country, government put economic reforms as forefront of its work. The central element of this approach included the pragmatism in regulation and implementation of foreign policy according to the values of Islam. In fact, practical line of Iran's foreign policy during the second decade after the revolution can be seen as the one with priorities to national interests, regional issues, avoiding provoking other countries in the framework of the policy of normalizing relations[228]. Although political elites insisted on some ideal aspects that can be realized in specific circumstances, in the same time accepting elements of realism in Iran's foreign policy to secure national interests and peaceful coexistence was constant. The political elites accepted the fact that there are several civilizations having culture, morals, races and nationalities, and in these conditions where all the countries follow principles of realism in their foreign policy, the best choice would be the policy of normalization, negotiation and communication. The necessity of turning an economy war system into a free market economy and rebuilding the country requires formation of government of Hashemi Rafsanjani. On the other hand, the transition from the level of an ideological cabinet to a

---

[228] Nia M. M. Title: A Holistic Constructivist Approach to Iran's Foreign Policy // International Journal of business and social science, 2011. [electronic source]. Available at: http://ijbssnet.com/journals/Vol._2_No._4;_March_2011/31.pdf (reference date: 11.04.2016).

technocratic one imposes new conceptions on the elite's interpretation of political concepts. Among these concepts and the most important development was the discussion of national interests. Following the decisions and recommendations of the General Assembly and the UN Security Council, adopting a supportive policy of Kuwaiti sovereignty in the war with Iraq, attempting to unite with moderate Arabs and identifying Iraq as an aggressor in the war with Iran by the United Nations in December 1991 could be seen as the result of the new regional leaders and international behavior of Iran that began in 1989. The most distinguished representation of the policy is the normalization of relations is based on national security and various meetings of the president and minister of foreign affairs with political personalities and foreign countries. Hashemi Rafsanjani has participated in 33 foreign trips during his two presidential terms, which is roughly equivalent to a trip per season. These trips have contributed to the recognition of the main actors of the international system and the introduction of Iran and its needs to other countries. It must be noticed that there was adherence to the principles of the constitution and protection of Muslims in the world. And despite achievement of Islamic ideas, commitment to Muslims and defense of their rights during this period, as it was in the past, its fundamental place in foreign policy was maintained. The Islamic republic of Iran provided and fulfilled them according to its capabilities. In other words, decision-makers and foreign policy implementers of the Islamic Republic in these years came to the conclusion that other countries should also considered as the ones representing the interests of their nations. Therefore, the policy of paying more attention to the external environment and participation in the ruling international system replaced the policy of avoiding the international environment that was prioritized during the Iran-Iraq war. In fact, foreign policy implementers of the Islamic republic during the years of presidency of Hashemi Rafsanjani were especially oriented to the necessities of the country in economy and politics[229]. In order to achieve the desired goals as well as satisfy the economic needs the idealistic policy of the time when Mir Hossein Mousavi was the Prime Minister was replaced by the more effective one. In other words, the necessity to pay attention to economic and security issues, providing national interests in the economic sphere has led Iran to pursue a pragmatic policy and coexistence with others in order to gain credibility and power. The pursuit of this policy required following mechanisms: acceptance of the ruling order of international relations, respect for international rules and principles, active participation in regional and international organizations, effort to create space for coexistence with others, especially cooperation with

---

[229] Sarmadi H., Badri M. The Effect of Hashemi Rafsanjani's Technocrat Government and changing of foreign policy of Iran from power to pragmatism // Academia Journal of Educational Research, 2017. [electronic source]. Available at: https://www.academiapublishing.org/journals/ajer/pdf/2017/Feb/Sarmadi%20and%20Badri.pdf (reference date: 01.11.2017).

neighboring and European countries to avoid bottlenecks and economic crises after revolution and Iran-Iraq war. Of course, it is important to mention that paying attention to economic issues was the factor of changing the foreign policy. Other factors such as necessity of restoring the country's military power, which was weakened due to eight years of war with Iraq, attention of foreign policy executives (implementers) to the special aspects of geopolitics of Iran have played a key role in changing the behavior of the country and its relations with others. In brief, understanding political elites from viewpoint of world politics during the eight years of Iran-Iraq war and presidency of Hashemi Rafsanjani was more based on geopolitics than on ideology[230].

In general, the foreign policy of the period of Hashemi Rafsanjani (so called period of construction[231]) can be summarized as following:

1) Necessity of paying attention to the economic and social issues and following national interests in the economic sphere has led to achieving credibility and power, following expediency policy and coexistence with others;

2) Acceptance of ruling order in international relations;

3) Respect of international rules and order;

4) Active membership in regional and international organizations;

5) Approaches to create coexistence space with neighbors and friendly countries;

6) The policy of exporting the revolution, which during the war was a cornerstone of foreign policy, turned into a policy of Islam in one country during the period of construction.

The so-called course of 2nd Khordad[232] (government of Seyyed Mohammad Khatami)

In this period détente policy was put on the agenda. This can be explained in a way that using of power in resolving international issues was replaced by using of peaceful means through bilateral and multilateral negotiations. Meanwhile, this policy should not allow ideological differences and political views to affect relations between countries. "Détente policy[233] in the framework of greatness, wisdom and expediency means that Iran in its foreign policy seeks to eliminate misunderstandings from the past and strive to put an end to any kind of dispute and international conflict, and to draw attention on international realities for its security."[234]

---

[230]Mohammad-Ali Hosseinzadeh, Governing discourses over government after revolution in Islamic Republic of Iran, Documentation Center of Islamic revolution.

[231] Government construction - Presidency of Akbar Hashemi Rafsanjani (the 5th and 6th government of Iran).

[232] The government (movement) of 2nd Khordad mean Presidential elections in Iran in 1997 and the Presidency of Mohamamd Khatami was the 7th and 8th government of Iran after the Iranian Revolution. At that time, Mohammad Khatami was president.

[233] Détente is the easing of strained relations, especially in political situation.

[234] Ibid.

The coast of hostility to the Islamic revolution should not be reduced at the level of governments and nations, but we much act in a way that hostility to Iran and the Islamic Revolution goes along with a serious material and spiritual (moral) cost for them. And for the reason of this high cost, countries will not be hostile to the Iranian revolution. About this policy of détente Khatami also stated: "The art of true diplomacy is that moment to moment we will reduce the number of our enemies and moment to moment the number of our friends and associates will be increased. Making an enemy your friend is a real art and Islamic republic of Iran as well as Ministry of foreign affairs always uses diplomacy based on following of the national interests. From a stage of détente policy[235] we will enter a confidence-building and from this confidence-building we will reach mutual cooperation and comprehensive regional integration." Based on a policy of détente Islamic republic of Iran considers having four main priorities for itself:

1)   Peace and security in neighboring countries of Iran;

2)   Maintenance of friendly relations with all the Islamic countries;

3)   Political, cultural and economic cooperation with selected (preferred) countries and organizations;

4)   Active participation in international organizations.

Dialogue among civilizations[236] is also in a line with the government of the Islamic Republic and follows policy of détente[237]. Khatami rejects the clash of civilizations and supports principle of dialogue between religions, cultures and nations. He believes in interdependence of societies, cultures and economics and supports kind of creative and stable foreign policy. According to him, this foreign policy must be based on avoiding violence and establishing friendly relations with all countries, so that they recognize the independence of Iran and an aggressive policy is not followed[238].

In Rouhollah Ramezani view foreign policy of Iran in that period was based on three main pillars. The first one is elimination of containment, the second – deterrence, the third – détente

---

[235] The détente policy - a strategy in Iran's foreign policy that began with the second term of Akbar Hashemi Rafsanjani and received a special attention during the presidency of Seyyed Mohammad Khatami. Hassan Rouhani also put forward a second wave of this policy. It is based on building trust between nations, resolving misunderstandings, economic pluralism, peaceful coexistence, etc.

[236] Former Iranian president Mohammad Khatami introduced the idea of Dialogue Among Civilizations as a response to Samuel P. Huntington's theory of a Clash of Civilizations.

[237] Esfahani A.S. Cultural Globalization and Foreign Policy Strategies of the Islamic Republic of Iran (Case Study; the Seventh and the Ninth Governments) // Published by Canadian Center of Science and Education, 2017. [electronic source].   Available   at: https://www.google.ru/url?sa=t&rct=j&q=&esrc=s&source=web&cd=1&ved=0ahUKEwjwka3ggKDXAhUHD5oKHXk 2CVAQFggnMAA&url=http%3A%2F%2Fwww.ccsenet.org%2Fjournal%2Findex.php%2Fjpl%2Farticle%2Fdownload %2F68640%2F37320&usg=AOvVaw0rQsqrbuNQ6d5KmxPqhkaE (reference date: 30.06.2016).

[238] Ibid.

policy. At first the government of Khatami was trying to relieve Iran from difficult political, military and ideological containment of the United States. Then, he tried to pay attention to Iran's important strategic position in the region, strengthen its defense position and deterrence. In the third place using détente policy he also tried to eliminate the conflicts between Iran and the countries of the region as well as the neighboring countries in the form of initiatives such as the dialogue of civilizations at the level of international organizations, especially the United Nations.

In general, principles of Iran's foreign policy during the policy-oriented developmental period can be summarized as follows:

1)   Détente policy and efforts to build trust at the regional and international levels;

2)   Emphasis on dialogue and communication between cultures in order to resolve issues and discussed problems at the level of foreign policy;

3)   Efforts to neutralize anti-Iranian policies by active participating in international conferences and assemblies for earning prestige at the international level;

4)   An attempt to recognize Islamic civilization as a civilization seeking peace, justice and dialogue in international relations;

5)   Trying to attract and use potential and capabilities of Iranians living abroad;

6)   Foreign policy making paying attention to capabilities and international obstacles[239].

Iran and the Arab countries

Among the geopolitical regions place of which in international system was developed, the region of southwestern Asia, especially the Middle East has always been of interest to the international system. The improvement of the relations between Iran and the influential Arab countries of the region during the time of Khatami government indicates that each side has changed its attitude. The Islamic Republic of Iran considers creation of good relations with Saudi Arabia as better relations with all Islamic countries in general and the Gulf states in particular. In this period, Iran has significantly increased its relations with the Arab countries. Existence of different cultural, economic and security ties among the countries of the Persian Gulf gave the Islamic Republic the opportunity to significantly increase its relations with the Arab and Muslim countries in the framework of the Islamic Conference, to help adjudicate the rights of the Palestinians, and to return to original Islamic culture[240].

---

[239] Ibid.
[240] Clawson P., Eisenstadt M., Kanovsky E., Menashri D. Iran under Khatami: a political, economic, and military assessment // The Washington Institute for Near East Policy, 1998. [electronic source]. Available at: https://www.washingtoninstitute.org/uploads/Documents/pubs/IranUnderKhatami.pdf.pdf (reference date: 01.05.2016).

Among the most important achievements of the détente policy are relations of Iran with Saudi Arabia that is basis of the balance and also key to communication with other Arab countries of the region. In this period Iran and Saudi Arabia have witnessed the warmest political ties during seventy years of their political history. Dialogue within the civilization with Islamic countries, through the emphasis on the regional Islamism, can be very effective for relations. It is likely that the most important help the summit did for creating foreign policy of conciliation was an unexpected opportunity for a mutually reinforcing dialogue between Arab and Arab states, including Saudi Arabia, the United Arab Emirates, Egypt, Iraq, Saudi Arabia, and others. One of Iran's main goals was creation of trust and confidence in relations with all the neighbors in the Persian Gulf region. The foreign policy of Iran towards the region in the period of Khatami governance was based on coalition and regional partnership[241]. In other words, during this period the Islamic Republic of Iran, by emphasizing realistic agreement, avoiding radicalism in foreign policy and resolving misunderstandings tried to accept (adopt) policies and common policies in relation to the region and common issues, regional countries, especially of the Persian Gulf. Therefore, regional relations of Iran with the Islamic countries were carried out in order to maximize regional cooperation and achieve coalitions. In this period apart from the positive effects of changes in Iran's foreign policy based on (the policy of détente), building trust and regional participatoryism (partnership), there was failure of the peace talks in the Middle East to change the policy of Arab countries, especially the countries of the Persian Gulf region towards Iran. In the same time Sheikh, King of Bahrain, Hamad bin Isa Al Khalifa had a formal official visit to Tehran in late August 2002, which was considered to be important. Relations between Iran and Saudi Arabia during the presidency of Khatami developed in political, educational, economic and security fields. In particular, with the visit of Khatami and other officials, including the visit of the Minister of Defense of Saudi Arabia, bilateral and multilateral cooperation between Tehran and Riyadh was exercised. They even adopted OPEC coordination policies on pricing and oil production. From their point of view, joint security cooperation in an area containing at least 60 percent of the world's oil reserves is necessary.

Analysis of the foreign policy of Iran during the presidency of Mahmoud Ahmadinejad

Period of idealistic principle (as the main axis) (1384-1392=2005-2013): domination of the discourse of idealistic principle on foreign policy of the Islamic Republic of Iran in this period can be attributed to many internal and international factors[242]. Iran's nuclear issue, increasing

---

[241] Ibid.
[242] Sadeghi B., Tabatabai S.M. Op.cit.

international pressure because of this, multiple inspections of the International Atomic Energy Agency (IAEA) representatives in the active centers for nuclear processing in Iran are seen as one of these factors. As President Ahmadinejad has often criticized Khatami's great retreat and policy of appeasement in his speeches, he insisted on the country's nuclear rights. Radicalization of policy-oriented developmentalism in a form of neglect of the fundamental principles of the Islamic Revolution and promotion of a kind of relativistic pluralism in society, which, in their minds, called into question a number of principles, can be seen as another reason.

President Ahmadinejad's re-emphasizing of Israel on the world map at the International conference on holocaust in Tehran in the presence of a number of foreign and domestic scholars was confirmed by the principles of the Islamic revolution, which is based on opposition to the United States and Israel[243]. Ahmadinejad has repeatedly pointed out the issue of disappearance of Israel in his official domestic and international statements including the organization of the United Nations (UN) and even at the International Conference of the World Food and Agriculture Organization (FAO) at its headquarters in Rome. Support of the Hamas movement and the Lebanese Hezbollah has also completely opened its doors in the official dialogues and speeches of the Presidency and other executive officials of the Republic. Although many international policy thinkers believe that there is no need to preserve national interests, declarative policies of a state are one thing with applicable policies at the level of foreign policy. Thus, one can reaffirm the ideals of the Islamic Revolution and emphasize its principles from the main characteristics of the principle of idealism of the foreign policy of the Islamic Republic of Iran. In this regard, at the level of foreign policy of Iran during this period, we are witnessing the expansion of Iran's foreign relations with the littoral south countries of the Persian Gulf - despite the border disputes. In addition to an active and comprehensive presence in the Gulf Cooperation Council, Ahmadinejad officially announces his request to attend the Arab League, as friendly and Muslim countries. Opposition to hegemonic unilateralism of the United States at the regional and international levels is another characteristic (factor) of this period of foreign policy of the country[244]. Based on this quite a few things in foreign policy political behavior of Ahmadinejad can be explained. Expansion of ties with the countries of Central and Latin America, opponent to the United States, active participation (membership) in the Shanghai Cooperation Organization (SCO) summit, demand for the transformation of Iran from an observer to a permanent member, offer of the formation of gas OPEC (the Gas Exporting Countries

---

[243] Hafezi P., Sedarat F. Ahmadinejad says Holocaust a lie, Israel has no future, 2009. [electronic source]. Available at: http://www.reuters.com/article/us-iran/ahmadinejad-says-holocaust-a-lie-israel-has-no-future-idUSTRE58H17S20090918 (reference date: 08.08.2016).
[244] Haghighat S. S. Op.cit.

Forum (GECF)) and east-oriented policy in Iran's foreign policy in this period can be analyzed in a form.

In relation to the recent issues, it is worth mentioning that we have seen three approaches and strategies in relation to the great powers. The first approach is looking at the West (West orientation), according to which the most important axis of Iranian foreign policy was group interacting with the West. From this point of view, interaction with non-West countries should be function of the approach of the West. They believe that orientation of Iran towards the East and alliance with powerful Asia countries – usually China and Russia can provide Iran's national interests and solve the problem of the lack of a strategic alliance for Iran.[245] The third approach stands against the two mentioned above approaches and is known as Neither East nor West, which believes in adopting a kind of negative-balance policy towards East and West. The discourse of idealistic principle with an emphasis on the policy of looking at the East (East orientation) as its main foreign policy approach is that new policy of looking at the East is in fact a détente policy with new approach around axis of interactive and constructive engagement. Idealistic emphasis based on some ideals and the official announcement of these policies from official tribunes has met the implications at the national and international levels. Intensification of sanctions on the international level has caused issues and economic problems on the domestic level.

The principles of foreign policy of the Islamic Republic of Iran during the principle of idealism can be summarized as following:

1)   Resisting and insisting on the country's nuclear rights and elimination of problems caused by it;

2)   Disclaimer and activity with US unilateral policies at the international and especially regional level

3)   Emphasis on the ideals of the Islamic Revolution, including the disappearance of the Israeli regime from the political map of the world;

4)   Support of resistant, revolutionary and freedom movements in Lebanon and Palestine;

5)   Adopting an approach to the East orientation in foreign policy and proximity to China and Russia;

6)   Impact of foreign policy approaches on ideological imperatives over the changes in the international environment;

---

[245] Azizian N. Russia & Iran: Strategic Alliance or Marriage of Convenience // Small Wars Journal, 2013.

7) Expansion and deepening of relations with neighboring countries, especially the Arab countries littoral south countries of the Persian Gulf;

8) Designing and presenting discourses in the international arena, including "culturalization of politics" and "governance of morality and spirituality" in global relations;

9) Axial justice and justice of development;

10) Spirituality (morality)[246].

It seems that this period in foreign policy of the Islamic republic of Iran can be better explained by the idealistic liberal ideas, because the emphasis of Ahmadinejad's government can be really reproduced by the production of foreign policy of Iran during the period of expansionist idealism. With the difference that the goal of foreign policy of Iran was more than development and expansion of the Islamic republic, which was only seeking to create anti-unilateralism of the United States at the international level by accepting Umm al-Qura's priority over other countries. It is clear for the countries negotiating with Iran. Also, in this period of time foreign policy of Iran is first of all influenced by idealistic policy based on some series of principles, rather than by the realities and international implications. This shows that the international norms may less likely affect the foreign policy of the country.

Advantages of Iranian foreign policy during this period

According to various statements of the Supreme Leader of Iran, he considered one of the strengths of this government to be the positions of the president and government members in foreign affairs. The same is true in terms of promoting the status of the country in the field of foreign policy and international affairs. Today in the field of foreign policy, the importance and weight of the country differs from the ones a few years ago; we influence the issues, this is what important... Another part of these strong points, which, in his point of view, should be relied on, is the issue of highlighting the values of the revolution. Fortunately, during the ninth and tenth governments until very this day, the discourse of the revolution, its values and what was explained by Imam and learnt from the revolution, was completely highlighted: the simple issues as authorities, resistance, pride of revolutionism.[247]

The revival of the resistance in the ninth government

Resistance has a meaning that comes from Islamic revolution have found its importance and clarity...The issue of restoring national dignity and the quitting of passivity against the domination

---

[246] Ibid.
[247] Leader Meets with Government Officials, 2013. [electronic source]. Available at: http://english.khamenei.ir/news/1807/Leader-Meets-with-Government-Officials (reference date: 08.08.2016).

and aggression and excessive policies of others and leaving westernization is also felt in this state; national dignity, true and spiritual (moral) independence are obtained here[248].

Resistance in the field of nuclear energy

During this resistance policy, there was a growth in scientific and practical capabilities of nuclear enrichment from 3.5 percent to 20 percent, increasing the number of active centrifuges, opening the first phase of the Bushehr nuclear power plant and increasing the opportunities of Iranian academics to exercise atomic energy in the pharmaceutical, medical, and agricultural sectors[249].

Foreign policy theorists of the ninth and tenth governments believe that the system of international relations is based on injustice so these countries are powerful as they influence in international structures such as the United Nations, the Security Council, etc. and must respond to their inefficiencies in world governance. This belief comes from the speeches of Ahmadinejad, which was expressed in 2005 and shows a new foreign policy of Iran. Policy that was later called "Offensive diplomacy". The period, when some supposed they were superior to others is over. Great powers should come down from their ivory tower and not talk with the Iranian nation from the position of arrogance. "In the offensive policy defense is not the main purpose, rather, it points out insufficiencies in the claiming countries fall within the framework of the rules of this type of diplomacy. In this case, it can be reminded about the government of European countries and violation of human rights, demand for a research on the human rights situation in the United States and appropriation to show disappointment of the Western countries people.

Also:

1)   Influence in America's so called "private place" (Latin America) and to a lesser extent in Africa;

2)   Holding Non-Alignment conference with the presence of Secretary-General of the United Nations and assume chairmanship of it;

3)   Smoothing the anti-Iranian case of the AMIA bombing attack in favor of Iran which had been broadcast for more than fifteen years as an international media propaganda campaign;

4)   Affective participation in victories in the 2006 Lebanon war (2006 Israel-Hezbollah War), the Gaza War (Operation Cast Lead), eight-day war (Operation Pillar of Defense) Islamic resistance to Israel;

5)   Establishment of a gas OPEC (Gas Exporting Countries Forum);

---

[248] Ibid.
[249] Ibid.

6)   Challenging the norms of crime/guilt commitment in international system (for example Holocaust);

7)   Foreign policy orientation towards the East and revival of the policy orientation towards the South. Thus, he ninth government uses policy of looking to the East as a strategy to establish balance. However, looking at the East does not mean ignoring the West. It means that we can use the weight of the East, especially of such countries as Russia, China, India, and even the countries of Southeast Asia, which are called industrialized countries. The policy of looking at the south has been taken into consideration in the face of North domination. It is aimed at the southern countries of Africa and Latin America. The observer membership of Iran in the African Union and support of the Zimbabwean people's struggle led by Robert Mugabe against British and American policies and also support of anti-colonial, anti-imperialist struggles in such countries as Cuba, Bolivia, Venezuela express a strategic look for political, economic and cultural changes in the international arena and use of international opportunities in direction of national interests; in particular, these countries had a plan called "Alba", and have been struggling to confront the American plan "Alca"[250] (to create free trade) and neoliberalism in the region. From this perspective, with the policy of looking at the South there is an anti-resistance front to confront the colonial politics of the northern powers and negation of the domination system of the world.

8)   Particular attention to creation of balance of the rights and duties in the field of international politics;

9)   As the diplomatic achievements of Iran in the context of non-alignment the following may be noted: the Joint Statement by the Non-Aligned Troika Foreign Ministers in November 2005 in Tehran and in 2006 in South Africa, the Declaration of the Ministers of Foreign Affairs of the Movement in Malaysia in May 2006, the Statement by the leaders of the Non-Aligned Movement in Cuba in September 2006 in support of Iran's nuclear rights;

10)   The signing of the contract for the establishment of a joint oil refinery in Syria, with the participation of Iran, Syria, Malaysia and Venezuela, as well as the opening of joint projects between Iran and Syria in the area of automobile industry and cement was part of the Foreign Ministry's agenda. Meanwhile, with regard to the normalization of relations between Iran and Egypt, Iran-Egypt meetings and efforts were taken to overcome obstacles and improve political relations;

11)   Strong support for liberation movements, such as Hezbollah (Lebanon).

---

[250] The Free Trade Area of the Americas was a proposed agreement to eliminate or reduce the trade barriers among all countries in the Americas, excluding Cuba.

The 11th cabinet of Islamic Republic of Iran (Government of Hassan Rouhani (2013 - 2017))

Rouhani promised to cure the unacceptable situation through the fundamental reform of the country's foreign policy. The changes he posed represent a realistic understanding of contemporary international order and current external challenges facing the Islamic Republic and also what is needed to bring Iran's relations with the outside world back to normal. Rouhani also called for moderation. This approach, in the same time as respecting national security, promoting the status of the country and achieving a comprehensive long-term development, seeks to lead Iran from confronting dialogue, constructive engagement and understanding. The moderation approach is based on realism, self-confidence, realistic idealism and constructive interaction. Necessity of realism is the perception of nature, structure, mechanisms and dynamics of power in international system as well as potential capacity and limits of its institutions. From the opinion of Rouhani, moderation is the combination of deep belief in the popular ideals of the Islamic Revolution with an objective assessment of the real capacities, abilities and limitations of Iran[251]. This encourages self-confidence based on an understanding of material and spiritual (moral) resources of Iran, including the collective wisdom of its citizens. This point of view puts value on accountability, transparency and honesty in dealing with people and implies preparation for the improvement of existing policies. Rouhani's approach requires a delicate effort in order to achieve the balance: between national, regional and global needs on one hand and possibilities, tools and existing policies on the other; between permanence and flexibility in foreign policy; between goals and possibilities; and between various tools of power in a constantly changing world. Finally, Rouhani's commitment to constructive engagement involves dialogue and interaction with other countries based on equal status, mutual respect and serving common interests. This approach requires other actors to make serious efforts to reduce tension, build trust and achieve the policy of détente.[252]

Considering the immediate challenges Iran will also focus on many urgent purposes. The priority is to neutralize and ultimately defeat the international anti-Iranian trend, which came from Israel and its American supporters; whose goal is "to secure" Iran. The main tool for this is the crisis over Iran's peaceful nuclear program; a crisis that, from the viewpoint of Iran, is completely fictitious and therefore in the end can be reversed. For this reason, Rouhani in order to break the

---

[251] Adib-Moghaddam A. Iran and the world after Rouhani // University of London, 2017-2018. [electronic source]. Available at: http://www.ide.go.jp/library/Japanese/Publish/Periodicals/Me_review/pdf/201709_01.pdf (reference date: 02.11.2017).
[252] Foreign policy of Iran during the period of Hatami in the words of Zarif, 2014. [electronic source]. Available at: http://www.yjc.ir/fa/news/4813696 (reference date: 01.01.2016).

deadlock and enter into negotiations with the P5 + 1 (China, France, Russia, the United Kingdom, and the United States; plus Germany) to find a common ground and reach an agreement, which guarantees non-proliferation, save maintains Iran's scientific achievements, pays respect to unalienable rights of the country based on the Treaty on the Non-Proliferation of Nuclear Weapons and puts an end to the unfair sanctions imposed by foreign powers. Iran does not have interest in nuclear weapons and is convinced that such weapons will not strengthen its security. Iran does not dispose the necessary means to enter nuclear deterrence against its enemies, either directly or indirectly. In addition, the Iranian government believes that even the perception that Iran is pursuing nuclear weapons is detrimental to the security of the country and its regional role, because Iran's attempt to achieve strategic superiority in the Persian Gulf will inevitably lead to incitement of reactions that will reduce Iran's conventional military superiority in the region. Therefore, ongoing talks on the nuclear issue do not confront the unacceptable obstacles. The requirements for success are merely determined by the political will and negotiators' goodwill to reach an agreement and achieve the goal set out in the Joint Plan of Action (JCPOA) adopted in Geneva in November last year, which states: "The goal for these negotiations is to reach a mutually-agreed long-term comprehensive solution that would ensure Iran's nuclear program will be exclusively peaceful".[253] The unexpected progress in the negotiations at the first phase is a positive sign of a quick resolution of this dispensable crisis and opening new diplomatic horizons. Iran will also try to remove foreign threats by resolving delayed issues with the rest of the world, especially with its immediate neighbors. Trust and cooperation will form the basis of Iran's regional policy. For the same reason, last year Iran proposed the establishment of the system of security and cooperation in the region of the Persian Gulf. Iran, being a responsible regional actor, will actively participate in the fight against extremism and violence and its limits through bilateral, regional and multilateral cooperation with the countries of the region and beyond. In addition, Iran will wisely manage its relations with the United States by limiting existing differences in views and tensions, avoiding appearance of more unnecessary ones, so that little by little tensions will be reduced. Iran will also interact with the countries of Europe and other Western countries with the goal of reestablishing the previous relations and its further development. This normalization process should be based on mutual respect and interests should deal with issues of legitimate interest of the parties. Iran will also strengthen and expand its friendly relations with other major powers such as China, India and Russia. Iran, which until 2015 held the presidency in the Non-Aligned Movement (NAM), and will try to

---

[253] The Iran nuclear deal: full text, 2013. [electronic source]. Available at: http://edition.cnn.com/2013/11/24/world/meast/iran-deal-text/index.html (reference date: 01.05.2016).

mobilize in responsible ways the huge potential capacities of the world developing countries in order to help bring peace and world prosperity.[254] Iranian people through their huge presence in the presidential election last year and a decisive vote of constructive engagement have provided an exceptional opportunity for the new government in Iran and the world to draw a different and much more hopeful way in our bilateral and multilateral relations. The Islamic Republic of Iran is determined to seriously respect the citizen's option, which will undoubtedly have a great impact on the affairs of the world. In order for this attempt of Iran to have success, it is necessary for other governments to accept the reality of Iran's prominent role in the Middle East and beyond, recognize and respect the national rights as well as legitimate security interests of Iran. It is also very important that other governments carefully observe the sensitivities of the Iranian people, especially in relation to national dignity, independence and achievements. The West, especially the Americans, need to correct their understanding of Iran and the Middle East and get a better understanding of the realities of the region in order to avoid analytical and practical mistakes of the past. It is essential with the courageous management of this historic opportunity, which may happen again, should be used to advantage. This opportunity should not be missed.[255]

[254] Diaz Sanz M. The Geopolitical Challenge of the Non-Aligned: Iran 2012-2015 // E-International Relations, 2012. [electronic source]. Available at: http://www.e-ir.info/2012/09/26/the-geopolitical-challenge-of-the-non-aligned-iran-2012-2015/ (reference date: 01.07.2016).
[255] Ibid.

3.2. Syria and Iran relations before and after the Arab spring in the Middle East

Relations between Iran and Syria are among the most prominent and are known for its continued existence. With the onset and continuing of the crisis in Syria, the importance of the relations between Iran and Syria, unlike in the past, is not merely bilateral and not based on a security and anti-Israeli issues. It can be said that efforts of the U.S., Israel, Europe and most governments in the Arab world have created a unite of these countries. These ties form a vast axis, including Iraq and Lebanon, what is called "axis of resistance" or a "golden belt".[256] The beginning of the Syrian crisis coincided with the Arab uprisings (Arab spring) in the late 2010s. Some foreign policy analysts think that the Syrian crisis is one of the same revolutionary movements as in the countries of the region. It should be mentioned that the relations between the two countries after the Islamic revolution, Syrian support of Iran in Iran-Iraq war, support for resistance in Lebanon and a memorandum of defense between Iran and Syria have put the Islamic Republic of Iran in a position where it could not ignore the terrorist invasion of such groups, as, for example, Al-Nusra front[257]. Further complexity of the conflict in Syria and the advances of the terrorist groups and the risk for Syrian president Bashar al-Assad called on Russia to demand direct military intervention on Syria to confront the terrorists of ISIL[258] and Al-Nusra. With the support of Iran Russia's military intervention in Syria has created another coalition, faced with regional and international actors opposed to the Syrian regime, such as the United States, Turkey and Saudi Arabia. The four-member coalition (including Russia, Iran, Iraq, and Syria) there was a block against the United States-led anti-ISIL coalition, which brought many regional and international consequences.[259] The Syrian considers to be the last bastion of the Arab states that is still opposing Israel. Syria supported Iran in the Iraq war against Iran for various reasons, and this fact (support of Syrian government while almost every other state supported Iraq) is still very valuable to Iran. The continuation of relations after the war has strengthened the union. Syria have also secured and guaranteed the presence of

---

[256] Drums Of War: Israel And The "AXIS OF RESISTANCE" (PDF // International Crisis Group, 2016. [electronic source] Available at: https://web.archive.org/web/20160304111425/http://www.crisisgroup.org/~/media/Files

[257] Al-Nusra Front or Jabhat al-Nusra , known as the Jabhat Fateh al-Sham (Arabic: transliteration: Jabhat Fataḥ al-Šām) after July 2016, and also described as al-Qaeda in Syria or al-Qaeda in the Levant, is a Salafist jihadist terrorist organization fighting against Syrian government forces in the Syrian Civil War, with the aim of establishing an Islamic state in the country. The group announced its formation on 23 January 2012.

[258] The Islamic State of Iraq and the Levant (ISIL, IPA: /ˈaɪsəl/), also known as the Islamic State of Iraq and Syria[note 1] (ISIS /ˈaɪsɪs/),[53] Islamic State (IS) and by its Arabic language acronym Daesh (Arabic: dāʿish, IPA: [ˈdaːʕɪʃ]), is a Salafi jihadist militant group and unrecognised proto-state that follows a fundamentalist, Wahhabi doctrine of Sunni Islam.

[259] Tabrizi A.B., Pantiucci R. Understanding Iran's Role in the Syrian Conflict // Royal United Services Institute for Defence and Security Studies, 2016. [electronic source] Available at: https://rusi.org/sites/default/files/201608_op_understanding_irans_role_in_the_syrian_conflict_0.pdf (reference date: 09.10.2017).

Iran in the Lebanese arena. This led to the emergence of Hezbollah, an escalation of the Islamic movement in the occupied Palestine and the exertion of pressure on Israel. For the above-mentioned reasons, the enemies of the resistance axis are trying to eradicate it with the escalation of the Syrian crisis. In this regard, Iran has been assisted with an active role in the foreign policy of Syria[260].

Meanwhile, the Islamic Republic of Iran seeks to keep the Shiites and Hezbollah, especially in Lebanon which responds to its national interests (geopolitical aspect, not ideological). It can be said that Iran's foreign policy in Syria is based on realism and maximum national interest. The development of the Syrian crisis in recent years has led to the convergence and unification of the two countries of Iran and Syria. It is partly because this crisis is a common threat to the security of both. As a Syrian strategic ally, Iran seeks to maintain the rule of Bashar al-Assad in Syria, and the two countries are seeking to create a balance between the represented threats[261].

The influence of the intervention of other regional countries in the Syrian crisis:

Since the beginning of the crisis in Syria, Tehran has focused on two threats: a military threat from Israel and the United States, and a threat from local rivals who are trying to undermine Iran's regional role. The direct threat posed to Iran by the United States and its allies exists because the possible change of the regime in Syria will also change the regional role of Iran (it will be greatly damaged). Meanwhile, regional rivals such as Saudi Arabia, Qatar and Turkey are struggling to challenge the regional plight of Iran through the Syrian crisis. The triple axis of Saudi Arabia, Turkey and Qatar intervened in the Syrian crisis to break the axis of Islamic resistance in Syria and advance their regional policies and on behalf of the major powers in the Middle East[262]. The three countries use the media, money and the support of the great powers in order confront the influence of Iran in Syria. What is interesting about the Saudi Arabia, Turkey and Qatar axis is that this political union pursues a new policy and this time, instead of supporting the two well-known Al-Nusra and ISIL, it now supports new radical alternative terrorist groups, such as al-Fatah. Of course, each of these three countries has its own specific objectives that they follow in Syria, but what is common is that they are opposing Iran's power in the region[263]. It should be mentioned that Iran's stance for Syria has a high cost. But it also should be underlined that the formed coalition against

[260] Keyhan B. The foreign policy of Iran in the Middle East // The publishing house of the Ministry of Foreign Affairs, 2015.

[261] Emami M. A. Policy and governance in Syria // Foreign policy quarterly, 1997.

[262] Farzandi A. Security of a ruling government in Syria for the Islamic Republic of Iran // Fars news agency, 2012. [electronic source]. Available at: www.farsnews.com/newstext.php?nn=13910614000696 (reference date: 03.02.2016).

[263] [electronic source]. Available at: http://www.tasnimnews.com/fa/news/1395/06/31/1191883 (reference date: 08.08.2017).

[264] Valdani J. Studying on the role of the Islamic Republic of Iran in Syria // Quarterly Journal on political studies, 2013.

Iran was shaped a long time ago. Thus, Turkey, which is a member of NATO, so it cannot be part of an alliance with Iran. Qatar has the largest amount of the U.S. bases in the country. The coalition formed against Iran is a set of new political conditions, most notably the Islamic awakening in the region, which threatens the interests of the United States.[264]

From the point of view of Iran, the United States, Britain and France do not have a desire to end the Syrian crisis, but tend to the defeat of ISIL and jihadi groups in areas of Syria (especially after the beginning of Russian air strikes), some countries in the region began to rethink their policies. In the same time one of the victories of Iran is the participation in Vienna along with the other powerful countries of the world. The analysts have argued that Iran's fundamental strategy toward the Syrian crisis has been challenged by the direct military intervention of Russia. The role of Iran is marginalized, and Russia may take its place. In this regard, it should be emphasized that Iran's and Russia's foreign-policy strategies towards Syria, although they provide the interests of the parties, have significant differences. The main goal of Russia can be stated as following: division of the sphere of influence and interests with the United States, especially after Iran's nuclear deal with world powers. In the same time Russia does not distinguish between terrorist groups in its own operations, in contrast to the American strategy based on the division of the region into different sects and groups and religions, and describes some terrorists as moderate and others as extreme. If Syria is under the influence of the United States, it will mean the expansion of the Takfiri war in the Muslim republics of Russia.

The purpose of the direct presence of Russian troops in Syria is to support the Syrian regime in securing its continuation on the Mediterranean coast, in order to allow the Western blockade against the Syrian regime to be broken in this region. Supporting of Bashar al-Assad as the strategic partner and preventing the establishment of a pro-western government in Syria is also important. The Iranian-Russian coalition in Syria is much more resistant than the US-backed coalition in Iraq in its fight against ISIL. Iran and Russia can complete the role of each other in Syria, still the Syrians themselves must decide on their own destiny. In fact, the purpose of both countries is one, but the benefits derived from this goal are different.[265] As for Iran, it has to be mentioned that the occurrence of any crisis near the borders of a country is one of the greatest challenges facing that country, especially if it is of a severe kind, with the basis of terrorism and extremism. In this regard, challenges facing Iran are the following: 1) Security. As a Shiite country, Iran must block any way that extremists penetrate the borders. On the other hand, the issue of the Kurdish population of Iran,

---

[265][electronic source]. Available at: http://p30lib.com/2017/10/08/ (reference date: 12.08.2017).

in the area where the Syrian and Iraqi Kurds are gaining strength, is directly linked to the security of the borders of the country, as it can be severely affected beyond the boundaries. 2) The military and economic costs. These costs increase with the prolongation of the crisis and the need to defend Iran's allies. The costs of the martyrdom of the Iranian forces should also be added to these costs. There are three basic views on the type of Iran's foreign policy approach towards Syria: 1) Human Rights Perspective. The viewers believe that the regime of Bashar al-Assad and the rule of the Ba'ath party in Syria have an undemocratic and unfair structure and that, during recent developments they have widespread human rights violations; 2) The ideological point of view. They believe that the current Syrian government is at the forefront of the region's resistance, and its strategic location is in the immediate vicinity of the resistance groups in Lebanon and the Palestinian territories, and since the fall Bashar al-Assad is in the queue of resistance, in all circumstances, there is a need to prevent the collapse of the Syrian government. 3) Geopolitical view. The supporters of this opinion believe that the Islamic Republic is a regional power and one of the components of Iran's supremacy is the political and security structure that governs this region. The building of power in the Middle East, the presence of resistance groups including Hezbollah, the strong current unity of the current Syrian government with the Islamic Republic, the Arab Spring have strengthened the Islamic republic's position. Therefore, the collapse of the Syrian government is in the interests of regional rivals and transnational opponents of the Islamic Republic. Regardless of the judgment of any of the above views and of what part of the public opinion, none of these views seem to be able to illustrate the Islamic Republic's foreign policy strategy in Syria alone. In the current situation, it is more rational to take a multi-layered and multidimensional strategy in Iranian diplomacy about the developments in Syria, which embraces the various aspects of the three above-mentioned perspectives[266]. Thus, it can be said that the role of the Islamic Republic of Iran as an influential actor in the development of Syria is important. The regional situation requires to find solutions to end the crisis in order to put an end to the terrible situation of Syria and to prevent the growth of terrorism in the destabilizing Syrian area.

3.3. Iran's foreign policy towards Syria and Saudi Arabia

The study of relations between Iran and Saudi Arabia, as the largest country in the Arab part of the Persian Gulf region is dependent on relations between Iran and the Arabs in general. Meanwhile, due to the central role of Saudi Arabia in the Middle East, the Persian Gulf, and among

---

[266] Niakui A., Behmanesh H. Opponent actors in the Syrian crisis: goals and approaches // Foreign relations quarterly journal.

Islamic countries, the type of Iran-Saudi relations has always been important in its peripheral environment. In other words, Saudi Arabia, as one of the members of the Arab community, has been always influence by the events of the region and the types of interactions of each country of the Persian Gulf region, the Middle East and Iran. Creating a climate of trust, understanding, distrust or misunderstanding between the two countries has had positive or negative effects in the region and the Islamic countries. Attention of Iran towards Saudi Arabia as one of the main actors in the region explains by such factors as the British withdrawal from the Persian Gulf region and the disruption of security resulting from this withdrawal on the one hand and the consequences arising from the Egyptian revolution and the revolutionary policies of Nasser in the region on the other. In other words, after the struggle to bring down Iran by the Arabs after the Egyptian revolution, it became clear that Iran and Saudi Arabia are countries, which may play a significant role in regional equations. Meanwhile, wariness of Iran that the region may be under the control of extreme Arab states such as Egypt, Syria, Iraq, Yemen leads to closer proximity between the two countries. In addition, the two-sided policy of the United States towards the region based on support of two countries Saudi Arabia and Iran, was coming along with the fears of the danger of influence of the Soviet communism, and once again it justified the need for further communication between the two countries. However, cautious policies of Saudi Arabia's in the region have also been effective in this regard. Consequently, despite the not-so-positive view on the relations between Iran and the Arab countries during the Pahlavi era, it should be noted that until the victory of the revolution the history of the two countries rarely had phases of hostility and coldness. The victory of the Islamic revolution in 1979 and the formation of the Islamic Republic of Iran opened a new chapter in bilateral relations. This victory of the Islamic Revolution is partly based on the Shi'ite revolutionary ideology, which was in contrast with the Sunni ideology of Saudi Arabia. In addition to the outbreak of the religious revolution in a monarchy, kingdoms of the region, and Saudi Arabia as one of them, were aware of the possible danger of their own security. Particularly due to the book of the revolution, these concerns were doubled. Policies and propaganda of the Western governments were used in kindling hostility and disagreements between Iran and Saudi Arabia[267].

Middle East regional order in the context of Arab disorders (2009-2017)

The Middle East regional order in a period of post-instability, based on a multi-polar power balance, and among governments is defined that are highly permeable to peripheral identities, which are the reasons of the ongoing conflicts over norms, regime legitimacy and behavior of other actors.

---

[267] Borujerdi A.H. Development of Arab-Iranian relations // Publishing house of Ministry of Foreign Affairs, Tehran. 2001, p. 145.

The multipolarity of this order is the basis for intergovernmental competition over security and hegemony of the region, which shapes the perception of the threat to its neighbors, especially in countries with a conflict of opinion. In this regard, according to some researchers, the role of identity differences in some of the countries of the region is considered to represent a bigger threat than competing armed forces. Firstly, because it is possible to exploit it as a means of external influence, overthrowing and challenging the legitimacy of other actors[268]. The Arab disorders has brought the regional of the Middle East into a new stage, called the "New new Middle East" or the "Third Arab cold war"[269]. The political situation of the region in the post-instability period has been the process that began in the 2000s and led to the polarization of the Middle East. International relations in the region after the events in 2011 can be seen with an intensification of sectarian gaps and an increase in the role of non-state actors. In general, the role of transnational identities in the Middle East in the discussed period is an indicator of the existing weakness of the state institution. Within this framework, sectarianism has become a political tool for regional hegemons, in addition to relation to affiliated groups in countries with deep ethnic-sectarian gaps, they have also influenced balance of power. The concept of sovereignty in the New Middle East comes from the gradual growth and development of the state as a social phenomenon in the context of history, but due to the colonial role in shaping the system of regional governments and the full support of political units it is partly artificial[270].

Implementation of sectarianism in the Middle East

An instrumental sectarianism as a component of regional order is a new phenomenon that has been accelerated by the U.S. intervention during the regional power struggle. On one hand, the 2010 Arab spring intensified the power struggles in the Middle East, and on the other hand, led to a bigger sectarianism instrumentation of the regional states. In other words, the presence of jihadists in countries experiencing uprisings due to sectarian sensitivities has led to an unprecedented spread of transnationalization of sectarian movements[271]. In addition, security concerns led to the proximity of the parties involved to the relevant social groups, and this combination along with ethnic

[268] Hinnebusch R. A. The sectarianization of the Middle East: Transnational identity wars and competitive interference. Project on Middle East political science (POMEPS) // University of St. Andrews. June 8–9, 2016. [electronic source]. Available at: https://pomeps.org/wp-content/uploads/2016/09/POMEPS-studies-21-transnational_Web-REV.pdf (reference date: 13.03.2017).
[269] Hinnebusch R. A. The sectarian revolution in the Middle East // Aloysius. In: R/Evolutions: Global Trends & Regional Issues, 2016.
[270] Shaw M. Sociological approaches to international relations // University of Sussex, UK, 2009.
[271] Narbone L., Lestra M. The Gulf Monarchies beyond the Arab spring: changes and challenges // Florence : European University Institute, 2015 [electronic source]. Available at: http://cadmus.eui.eu/handle/1814/37734 (reference date: 12.08. 2016)

cleansing and the domination of sectarian discourse on television and social media intensified sectarianism in the Middle East after a period of uprisings. Therefore, the role of transnational Arab and Islamic identities in the sectarian format continues to be their state form through Iran and Saudi Arabia. For Saudi Arabia, which was once a tough opponent of pan-Arabism, the Syrian war has become a symbol of it, so that influence of Iran in the Arab lands is not acceptable, and according to its ideological tendencies represents their sphere of influence. On the other hand, Iran, which is the main actor of the opposition, intends to develop within the framework of the Pan-Islamist discourse by maintaining Syria as the last and only access point to Lebanon's Hezbollah at the forefront of confrontation with Israel[272]. Based on this, Arab and Islamic transnational identities in their new form have not only challenged government monopolies on communication networks but are instrumental in advancing the strategy of regionalized hegemonic governments. In this new order, regional actors are divided into two main groups. The first group includes the major regional actors such as Iran, Saudi Arabia and Turkey, which have powerful influence based on historical identity, material and human resources, and domination of the internal geographic units. In addition to this, they support domestic groups, have supranational ideological affinity, and the ability to provide financial assistance and arms. The second group is the majority of states with multi-sectarian communities in the Middle East and North Africa, such as Iraq, Syria, Bahrain, Yemen, and Libya, who have fallen victim to the new power struggle. Sectarianism has not only led to the polarization of the population in the above-mentioned governments, but also has led sectarian tendencies to be the basis for the opposition's form and coherence. According to Ibn Khaldun regimes rely more heavily on sectarian solidarity[273].

During the process of sectarianism in the Middle East, powerful states use different strategies. Saudi Arabia, which plays a key role in Sunni sectarianism, has introduced the Shiites as an atheist minority and emphasized the role of Iran as a non-Arab actor in the Arab world seeking to exploit the majority of the Sunni world against Iran. Contrary to that, the Islamic ideology discourse of Iran aims to rebuild Muslim resistance against the United States and Israel and their regional

[272] Khoury N.A. The Arab Cold War Revisited: The Regional Impact of the Arab Uprising // Middle East Policy 20 (2): 2013.

[273] Goldsmith L. (2011), Syria's Alawites and the Politics of sectarian Insecurity: a Khaldunian Perspective // Middle Eastern Studies. University of Otago. Volume 3, Pages 33-60 [electronic source]. Available at: https://www.researchgate.net/publication/281230449_Syria%27s_Alawites_and_the_Politics_of_Sectarian_Insecurity_A_Khaldunian_Perspective (reference date: 05.02.2017)

Kalin I. Sectarianism: A Recipe for Disaster for Sunnis and Shiites. 2014. [electronic source]. Available at: https://www.dailysabah.com/columns/ibrahim-kalin/2014/06/17/sectarianism-a-recipe-for-disaster-for-sunnis-and-shiites (reference date: 07.03.2016)

partners (led by Saudi Arabia). In contrast, Saudi Arabia uses Salafist elements and the Islamic Republic of Iran relies on the mobilization of the transnational network of Shiite minorities. Meanwhile, the gaps in the Sunni world (the confrontation between the Iraqi secularists and Islamists against Qatar and Turkey, Erdogan against Egypt during Abdel Fattah el-Sisi presidency) have led to a diminution of the Shiite minority's presence against the Sunnis of the Middle East[274].

Kingdom of Saudi Arabia (leader of the Holy Arab Alliance)

In general, the regional status of Saudi Arabia was in an unfavorable situation due overthrow Saddam Hussein in the 2000s and its position during the 2006 Israel-Hezbollah War (the July war). The negative results of the Arab uprisings have led to the collapse of the authoritarian and have changed the regional balance more favorably for the rivals. In this regard, Saudi Arabia, which throughout the history of the New Middle East has always been one of the main actors and leader of the Arab-Islamic for a considerable number of Arab countries, have formed a bloc of power together with other monarchies of the Cooperation Council for the Arab States of the Gulf. The goal of such policy was to confront the wave of uprisings in the member states and then promote their regional status[275].

Therefore, the orientation of the alliance against Arab uprisings and instabilities had dimensions: defensive and aggressive. Given the widespread scope of the uprisings that included such countries as, for example, Morocco (North Africa) and Oman (the Eastern state of the Arabic peninsula), the first members of the Holy Arab Alliance[276] called for annexation of other monarchies of the region to this alliance. In this regard, the Cooperation Council for the Arab States of the Gulf, as the core of the Holy Arab Alliance proposed to join the non-oil kingdoms of Jordan and Morocco[277].

It seems that the goals of such actions are adoption and implementation of coordinated policies by the kingdoms of the region, which helps standing against the uprising wave on one hand and to control and limit its scope on the other. In this regard, the Holy Alliance of Arab States incorporates a combination of methods, including the deployment of a military force to suppress the political protests of the reformers (Bahrain), granting political privileges and changing the constitution (Morocco), etc. The only difference was support of Qatar for the Egyptian Muslim

---

[274] Gause G. Beyond Sectarianism: The New Middle East Cold War // Brookings Doha Center. 2014 [electronic source]. Available at: (reference date: 12.03.2017)

[275] Gause G. Is Saudi Arabia really counter-revolutionary? // The Middle East channel // Foreign policy. 2011 [electronic source]. Available at: http://foreignpolicy.com/2011/08/09/is-saudi-arabia-really-counter-revolutionary/ (reference date: 16.03.2017)

[276] Holy Arab Alliance (HAA or Arab Alliance for short) is a political organization of multiple Arab countries.

[277] Koch C. Constructing a viable EU-GCC partnership // Gulf Research Center Foundation. 2014 [electronic source]. Available at: http://eprints.lse.ac.uk/55282/1/Constructing-aviable-U-GCC-relationship.pdf (reference date: 10.09.2017)

Brotherhood. From the regional point of view, the formation of the Holy Arab Alliance is part of the Saudi Arabia strategy to fill the empty space of its former allies, especially the ex-Egyptian president Hosni Mubarak. In relation to this, following the realization of the initial goal of unification and the end of the uprising wave in the member states, the goals were gradually moving in an aggressive way. In the following section, there is a summary on relations of some of the countries that have experienced Arab uprisings (Libya, Yemen, Syria) and Saudi Arabia in the frames of the Alliance. The Libyan government during the presidency of Muammar Gaddafi was selling weapons to Iran during the Iran-Iraq war as a part of balancing policies (1988-1989). His adventurous actions such as the assassination of King Abdullah, former king of Saudi Arabia, the disregard for Arab League decisions, etc. for most of Arab states in the region, the Middle East and North Africa has always been considered as those of an enemy and an undesirable element. Therefore, the uprisings in this country were an opportunity for the regional governments, and particularly the members of the Holy Arab Alliance, to get rid of Gaddafi. In this regard, after the uprisings in this country and Gaddafi loss of control of the parts of the country, Saudi Arabia and other monarchies used the mass media (Al Jazeera and Al Arabiya) and influence of their voices in the Alliance to stand against Libya[278].

Yemen is one of the other countries that, in the light of Arab uprisings, was the scene of Saudi intervention. On this basis, due to the weakness of civil society, the existence of ideological gaps along with the activities of radical Islamist groups has led to the government's severe inability to resist in Yemen. In this regard, major concern of Saudi Arabia as neighbor of Yemen were to stabilize the country and prevent the spread of uprisings in Saudi Arabia.[279] Following the spread of uncertainties and the split between the army and the central government in Yemen, the Saudi government, in pursuit of its historic role in this country, sought to secure security concerns. In this regard, plan of Gulf Cooperation Council (GCC) supported by the U.S. and European Union, provided mediation for the peaceful transfer of power from Yemeni President Ali Abdullah Saleh, president of Yemen during the uprisings to Abdrabbuh Mansur Hadi, was launched in 2012[280]. Even though the above-mentioned policies (in Libya and Yemen) are a sign of the success of the

[278] Filipkova L., Hesova Z., Karasek T., Kubikova N., Kuzvart J., Zahora J. NATO and the Arab Spring: challenge to cooperation,Opportunity for Action? // Association for International Affairs. 2012. [electronic source]. Available at: https://www.amo.cz/wp-content/uploads/2015/11/pp-2012-01.pdf (reference date: 10.09.2017).
[279] Matthiesen T. Transnational Identities after the Arab Uprising, in Luigi Narbone and Martin Lestra(eds), The Gulf Monarchies beyond the Arab spring: changes and challenges // Florence : European University Institute. 2015.
[280] Thiel T. After the Arab Spring power shift in Middle East?:Yemen's Arab Spring: from youth revolution to fragile political transition // LSE Research Online. London School of Economics and Political Science. 2012. [electronic source]. Available at: https://www.lse,ac.uk/IDEAS/publications/reports/pdf/SR011/FINAL_LSE_IDEAS_Yemen's Arab Spring_Thiel.pdf (reference date: 02.09.2017)

diplomatic apparatus of Saudi Arabia and the Council, these measures could not fill the empty space of their regional allies, especially Mubarak, who was thrown during the Arab uprisings. In this way, Syria has become an important part of the Saudi Arabia regional strategy; the uprisings in cities such as Daraa, Hama and Homs were a chance for this country to change negative response of Syria not to be represented in the opposition to join the American peace block and reduce the level of its relations with Iran.[281]

The given description represents the general policies of Saudi Arabia within the Holy Arab Alliance in the Middle East after the uprisings. This policy was changed in January 2005. During the reign of King Abdullah of Saudi Arabia, the country had few uprisings in its eastern provinces, in particular, the Al-Qatif (Shiite area), it followed the strategy of preserving the status quo and its offensive policy became quite limited. After the transfer of power from Abdullah bin Abdulaziz Al Saud to Salman bin Abdulaziz Al Saud, the foreign policy of this country became heavily offensive. In this regard, the new government of Saudi Arabia had cooperation within the framework of the Gulf Cooperation Council. It included such operations as "Decisive storm", "Restoring hope" on March 25, 2015 in Yemen, following the goal of limiting Shia Houthis on political arena of this country. It seems that such an offensive policy of Saudi Arabia and its allies was a reaction to US regional policy under the presidency of Barack Obama (2009-2017) and their support of Arab monarchies on one hand and ineffectiveness of the above-mentioned countries under the governance of Saudi Arabia in preventing conclusion a nuclear deal between Iran and the P5+1 (China, France, Russia, the United Kingdom, and the United States; plus Germany). Iran's withdrawal from international isolation by nuclear resolutions would increase its ability to engage in regional conflicts. Based on this, the regional changes have created the feeling that only the Arab states, and especially Saudi Arabia, unlike in the past, had to play their regional role alone and balance the position of Iran[282]. In this context, Saudi Arabia, knowing the importance of the role of identities in the Middle East, mainly Sunni, Sunni-Arab, tried to limit sectarianism in the area of the influence of Iran. This country considers all the Arab lands as its sphere of influence and considers Iran's proximity to the Shiite Iraqi government or Hezbollah's powerful organization in Lebanon as not unacceptable. In this regard, the Saudis pursued their activities at both regional and national levels to regulate influence of Iran. At the regional level, attack of Saudi Arabia on Yemen aimed at suppressing its Shiite minority is in fact a reaction to the regional role of Iran. This is followed by

---

[281] O'Bagy E. The free Syrian Army // Institute for the Study of War. 2013 [electronic source]. Available at: http://www.understandingwar.org/sites/default/files/The-Free-Syrian Army-24MAR.pdf (reference date: 06.09. 2017)
[282] Gause G. The Future of U.S – Saudi Relations: The Kingdom and the Power // Foreign Affairs. Volume 95, Issue 4. 2015.

the widespread mobilizing of opponents of Bashar al-Assad and especially the Islamists, who were active in the Syrian civil war. At the national level, Saudi Arabia recently aimed to violate internal security of Iran. So, the relations between the former and current officials of the country with Iranian opposition groups abroad (Kurdish separatists and the People's mojahedin organization of Iran) were the reason of decisive solutions of Saudi Arabia and its allies in the region to limit Iran[283]. Barack Obama, as the strategic partner of Saudi Arabia in the region, was also cautious against the U.S. involvement in what it calls proxy wars fueled by Saudi-Iranian competition in the Middle East, as, for example, in Yemen in Syria.[284]

Changing of power in the United States and presidency of Donald Trump as the forty-fifth president of the U.S., apparently, changed the attitude towards Saudi Arabia as well. In his pre-election campaigns, Trump strongly criticized Obama's Middle East policy, and in one of his speeches explicitly portrayed Saudi Arabia as as a "fat, and milky" cow[285]. In this connection, the regional policy of the United States of the new president is based on two pillars. The first one is to follow the old strategy of supporting its regional allies, particularly Saudi Arabia and Israel. The second one is the creation of a coalition between the countries of the region against Iran and the extremist Islamic movements. The choice of Saudi Arabia as the destination for the first foreign trip of Donald Trump shows its special position in maintaining regional stability and global economic security. The relationship between the two countries in the past years has been based on the doctrine of oil security. In other words, constant access to Saudi oil for the United States and the Saudi's support of the U.S. formed the basis of the mutual relations. Within this framework, after approximately two decades of tensions between Saudi Arabia and the United States during the presidency of George W. Bush and Barack Obama (2000-2016), the election of Donald Trump as president for the Saudi authorities means renewment of the partnership and restoring the U.S. commitment to Saudi Arabia. In order for Saudi Arabia to change regional equilibrium and reduce the role of Iran, they expect the U.S. to support three countries: Iraq, Syria and Yemen. In Iraq, the Saudi government wants a comprehensive government that is less focused on Shiite sectarian tendencies. The Saudis know that most of the Iraqi population is Shiites. Accordingly, there is no possibility of transferring power to the Sunnis, but the existence of a state with less sectarian

---

[283] Karami A. Saudi Prince's endorsement of MEK angers Iranian officials // AL-Monitor. 2016 [electronic source]. Available at: http://www.al-monitor.com/pulse/originals/2016/07/iran-mek-mojahedin-saudi-turki-bin-faisal.html (reference date: 10.09.2017)
[284] Schmierer R., Jeffrey J. F., Nader A. Nazer F. The Saudi-Iranian Rivalry and the Obama Doctrine // Middle East policy, Volume 23,Issue 2, 2016.
[285] Donald Trump: we should milk the fat Saudi Arabia as much as possible, and when the wealthy sheikhs become useless we should abandon the Middle-East // The World Observer. 2011. (reference date: 16.02.2016)

tendencies can reduce influence of Iran as the largest Shiite state in the region. On the contrary, since the majority of Syria's population is Sunnis, the Saudis are seeking to overthrow the rule of Assad and transfer power to other party. In this regard, the strategy of removing Syria from the Iranian influence, would disconnect Iran and Hezbollah from Lebanon. Eventually, the Houthis' defeat in Yemen and the transfer of power to Abdrabbuh Mansur Hadiare were Saudi Arabia's last steps aimed at overcoming the risk of regional influence in Iran. On one hand, the Saudi politicians wanted to strengthen the military power of this country with the help of the U.S., and on the other, not to let the presence of Iran in other Arab country of the Middle East region[286]. The trip of Donald Trump to Saudi Arabia on May 20, 2017, have led to a $ 110 billion to an establishment of arms sales contract. Along with the strict position of the U.S. towards Iranian missiles and presence of Iranian or affiliated Iranian forces (such as Liwa Fatemiyoun or Liwa Zainebiyoun) in Syria, there is a change of conditions in line with the demands of Saudi Arabia. However, these changes do not mean a complete change of policies against Iran. But it has cards that can be used in the new game and result in their favor.

The Islamic Republic of Iran

Before the beginning of Arab uprisings, the Islamic Republic of Iran, as the leader of the resistance block in the Middle East, was in a better position than other major regional actors. After the overthrow of Taliban in Afghanistan (2001), Saddam Hussein in Iraq (2003), for the first time after the Islamic Revolution, for the first time Iran was able to appear as a major regional actor, support Hezbollah in 2006 Lebanon War (the July war), and with some support of the Arab Middle East societies increase its soft power in the region. In this regard, the decade before the Arab uprisings was the period of the growth and consolidation of regional power of Iran in the Middle

East due to its success in Syria, Lebanon, Iraq and Palestine. In the beginning, the Iranian government viewed uprisings in the Arab countries with some skepticism and was considering this to be a way to weaken the Islamic countries, and especially Iran[287]. The rapid collapse of the secular and supported by the United States regimes in Egypt and Tunisia as well as the high role of Islamic movements in overthrowing these regimes have changed the attitude of Iranian authorities towards recent changed in the region, so that they interpreted these uprisings as the continuation of the Islamic Revolution of Iran and referred to it as "Islamic awakening".[288]

---

[286] Althunayyan H. The U.S.-Saudi relations in the Trump era // Aljazeera Media Network. 2017. [electronic source]. Available at: http://www.aljazeera.com/indepth/opinion/2017/05/saudi-relations-trump-era-170518084540044.html (reference date: 02.11.2017).
[287] Abu H. Firas. Iran and the Arab Revolutions: positions and Repercussions //Arab Center for Research and Policy Studies. 2011. [electronic source]. Available at: http://english.dohainstitute.org/file/get9a915419-721c-45ab-aa11-1cbac8dbaac3.pdf (reference date: 04.04.2016).

In this regard, in 2012, when the Arab uprisings have started, Iran hosted a significant number of the heads of the Arab-Islamic countries. Regarding the fact that the international pressure on Iran over its nuclear program was in the same time as the regional changes, it seems that the discussed uprisings were for an opportunity Iranian government to increase security and promote the regional status of the country. The moderate and opposing to the West Islamic parties helped to consolidate the regional position of the resistance axis as an independent block of power. If the Arab uprisings are considered to be only a series of revolutions, it is the product of the rivalry between the two main actors in the Middle East region – Iran and Saudi Arabia. Meanwhile, Bahrain and Yemen were the main battleground between the powers in terms of neighboring Saudi Arabia and the considerable number of Shiites. Regarding the uprisings in Bahrain, where more than 70 percent are Shiites and the country is under control of the Sunni minority, the Iranian government is primarily concerned of the the intervention of Saudi Arabia and the UAE armies along with other Arab countries (Jordan) and even the non-Arab (Pakistan) in region under the guidance of the security forces of the Cooperation Council for the Arab States of the Gulf, who severely suppressed the peaceful political protests.[289] In relation to this, members of the Holy Arab Alliance condemned Iran in interfering in the international affairs of their countries. Many of the Iranian media, such as Press TV, social media and radio were blamed by the Bahrani security agencies in supporting opposition to influence the situation in this country.[290] The report from January 22, 2011 of the Bahrain Independent Commission of Inquiry (BICI)[291] and the first king of Bahrain Hamad bin Isa bin Salman Al Khalifa declared that there was no such participation[292]. The geographical proximity of Bahrain to the Eastern Province (Ash-Sharqiyyah) and in particular the cities of Dammam, Al Ahsa and Qatif, where the biggest amount of Shiits live in the country, as well as the geopolitical significance of the area for the Saudis in terms of the presence of major Saudi oil supplies near it is a matter of concern for Saudi Arabia and other countries of the Holy Arab Alliance. It was explained by a possible takeover of power by the Bahraini Shiites, which could change the regional equilibrium and Iran's further expansion of regional influence over the last decade. Therefore, with

[288] Kurzman C.The Arab Spring: Ideals of the Iranian Green Movement, Methods of the Iranian Revolution // International Journal of Middle East Studies. Volume 44, Issue 1, 2012.
[289] Ulrichsen K. C. The Uprising in Bahrain: Regional Dimensions and International Consequences, in Larbi Sadiki(ed) // Routledge Handbook of the Arab Spring: Rethinking Democratization // New York: Routledge Taylor & Francis Group. 2015.
[290] Rivera J. Iran's Involvement in Bahrain // Small Wall War Journal. 2012. [electronic source]. Available at: http://smallwarsjournal.com/jrnl/iran%E2%80%99s-involvement-in-bahrain (reference date: 05.04. 2016).
[291] The Bahrain Independent Commission of Inquiry (BICI), also known locally in Bahrain as the Bassiouni Commission, was established by the King of Bahrain on 29 June 2011[1] tasked with looking into the incidents that occurred during the period of unrest in Bahrain in February and March 2011 and the consequences of these events.
[292] Mabon S. The Battle for Bahrain: Iranian-Saudi Rivalry // East Policy. Volume 19, Issue 2, 2012.

the knowledge of the role and position of supra-national identities in the region, these countries are trying to control the opposition. Yemen is among countries that, like most of the other Arab states, faced uprisings in 2011-2012. In 2016 the population of Yemen was roughly more than 27 million, of which 65 percent were Sunni and 35 percent Shiite. During the period of the spread of uprisings and the transfer of power in the country, intervention of Iran in Yemen and its support for the Zaidi Shiite minority were never discussed. But this matter was mentioned by members of the GCC after the Houthis dominated Sana'a and the disengagement of the President approved by Saudi Arabia in 2014. Despite Iran's support for the activities of Islamic movements, and in particular the Shiites in the region, the Houthis' actions were also surprising to Iran.[293] In the discussed theme it also should be mentioned that on the one hand Iran was involved of solving its nuclear deal, and on the other was worried about the rising power of the ISIS in Iraq and preserving power of Bashar al-Assad. In other words, despite the vision of the Arab governments, especially Saudi Arabia, of Iran as a country supporting the Yemeni Shiites, as well as the Houthi Islamic movements, Yemen was not the top priority for the foreign policy of Iran. The coincidence of the successes of Houthis in Yemen, the presence of the the Quds Force in Iraq and Syria sparked the feeling that the country was seeking expansionist policies in the region. Yet, unlike Yemen, Iraq, Syria and Lebanon have a much higher position in the vast orientation of Iran's foreign policy. The beginning of the arms supply by Iran of the Houthis was after their domination in the capital (September 2014), overthrow of Abdrabbuh Mansur Hadi (October 18, 2014) and his escape to his hometown of Aden when an agreement between Tehran and Sana'a was reached, so that there could be about 14 direct flights a week. At the same time, less than a month after the signing of the agreement, Saudi Arabia, along with the Arab coalition, launched an attack on Yemen and the interconnection between the two countries was effectively blocked. Despite the support of Iran for Shiites and, particularly, the Ansar Allah group in Yemen, the lack of response of this country to airstrikes of Saudi Arabia and the Arab coalition shows a lack of understanding of position of Yemen in the foreign policy of Saudi Arabia and to this point draws attention of Iranian politicians[294]. Statements of the Iranian authorities and their position showed in the case of Yemen the Iranian government did not want to oppose Saudi Arabia. Unlike Bahrain and Yemen, Egypt had a great importance in the regional strategy of Iran after the presidency of Hosni Mubarak. First of all, it was due to its geopolitical position in the Arab world

---

[293] Esfandiary D., Tabatabai A. Yemen: an Opportunity for Iran-Saudi Dialogue? //The Washington Quarterly. Volume 39, Issue 2, 2016.

[294] Mohseni P. Iran and the Arab World after the Nuclear Deal: Rivalry and Engagement in a New Era // Belfer Center for Science and International Affairs, 2015. [electronic source]. Available at: http://www.belfercenter.org (reference date: 22.08.2017).

close to Israel. In this regard, the Iranian government in the short period of Muslim Brotherhood (the Society of the Muslim Brothers) being a political power, wanted Egypt to establish friendly relations with the country. Mahmoud Ahmadinejad, the then president of Iran (2006-2012) visited the country for the first time since the victory of the Islamic Revolution during the reign of the first and only elected president of Egypt after the fall of Mubarak - Mohamed Morsi, Morsi as well was invited to the Non-Aligned Movement in Tehran[295]. In fact, there was no possibility to establish friendly relations between the two countries due to such factors as strong economic dependence of Egypt on the U.S. and the Persian Gulf monarchies, opposition of the Syrian Muslim Brotherhood to the rule of Bashar al-Assad, Iranian support of Mursi until the military coup d'etat in July 2013. Thus, overthrow of Morsi's government has never led to a deep-seated friendly relationship between the two countries[296].

According to Chapter X and particularly Article 154 of the Constitution of the Islamic Republic of Iran: "The Islamic Republic of Iran has as its ideal human felicity throughout human society, and considers the attainment of independence, freedom, and rule of justice and truth to be the right of all people of the world. Accordingly, while scrupulously refraining from all forms of interference in the internal affairs of other nations, it supports the just struggles of the Mustad'afun (oppressed) against the Mustakbirun (oppressors) in every corner of the globe".[297] Therefore, the interference in other country's affairs is not acceptable until it is the oppressed people. That explains the overall orientation of the foreign policy of this country, where there is no doubt that defending the Palestinian Muslim nation against Israel will be Iran's highest priority in international politics. In this regard, view of Iran on the uprisings in Syria is more focused on the country's position as the only state actor along with Iran in the resistance axis, so that the axis is currently the only bloc of unified power against Israel in the region. Therefore, Iran aims to adopt a sing united policy of the regional countries towards Israel. For Iran, helping to maintain secular rule of Bashar al-Assad is important because it has a connection role of Iran and Hezbollah in Lebanon. On the other hand, the two countries are sharing their stance on hostility to Israel[298].

As one of the superior powers of the region, Iran, like other key actors, wants to play a regional role, but this role is defined in the context of Islamic discourse. Just as Saudi Arabia today

[295] El-Labbad M. Egypt:A Regional Reference in the Middle East. In Henner Furtig(ed).Regional Powers in the Middle East: New Constellations after the Arab Revolts // New York: Palgrave. 2014.

[296] Hinnebusch R. The Arab Uprisings and the MENA Regional States System // Uluslararasi ilishikler. Volume 11, Issue 42, 2014.

[297] Iran (Islamic Republic of)'s Constitution of 1979 with amendments through 1989. [electronic source]. Available at: https://www.constituteproject.org/constitution/Iran_1989.pdf?lang=en (reference date: 06.06.2017).

[298] Maltzahn N. V. The Syria-Iran Axis: Cultural Diplomacy and International Relations in the Middle East // Library of Modern Middle East Studies // I.B.Tauris & Co Ltd. 2015.

has this tendency in the framework of Arabic discourse[299]. It should be noted that until the writing of the present study (December 2017) Syria stays a blind spot of the regional play between Iran and other countries of the Middle East.

Conclusion of the third chapter

In the third chapter author focuses on the fundamental features of Iran's foreign policy under the leadership of Imam Khamenei. The first part of this chapter emphasize the priorities and characteristics of Iranian foreign policy during the governments of Rafsanjani, Khatami, Ahmadinejad and Rouhani. It can be concluded that under Khamenei leadership each one of them had a separate policy. Thus, for example, Ahmadinejad was following the most controversial foreign policy of the confrontation with the Arab countries, while two of the previous presidents were the supporters of the détente policy focused on keeping peaceful relations with other countries. The second part examines relations of Iran and Syria before and after the Arab spring. It is said that Iran was supporting Syrian government with a realistic orientation of its point of view. The third part is about relations of Iran and Saudi Arabia. It has to be said that both of the countries aim to expand their influence in the region, as well as in the countries suffered from the Arab uprisings, they also want to be a part of the Greater Middle East. Due to the sectarian perspective, peace cannot be imagined in the region in the nearest future.

---

[299] Khalid A. Iran calls on Syrian President to consider protesters demands // Independent. 2011. [electronic source]. Available at: http://www.independent.co.uk/news/world/middle-east/iran-calls-on-syrian-president-to-consider-protesters-demands-2345536.html (reference date: 12.07.2016).

Conclusion

Therefore, the following conclusion can be made in the end of the research:

The author determined the structure of Iran's decision-making process and underlined the special features of it. The legal and political structure of foreign policy of the Islamic Republic of Iran can be expressed by the fact that the government's decisions on foreign policy are more likely to protect national interests. Religion and Islamic ideology formed the basis of the foreign policy of Iran, and according to Islamic principles it does not accept the domination and oppression of Muslims, and considers support for them as its duty. Because the fundamental factor in this discourse is religion or ideology, and not the geographical boundaries. From this point of view, the Muslim community is seen as Ummah. It is necessary to avoid the domination of others, to achieve unity and to form a global government. Therefore, these principles must be followed: 1. Independence. 2. Islamism. 3. Protection of other Muslims and Islamic unity. The foundations of Iran's foreign policy can be seen in the constitution, which, as explained in Chapter 1, is the preservation of existence in any system of primary and vital goals. At the beginning of the Islamic Republic these principles had a great importance to revolutionaries in its most ideal form. But the formation of the first government was choosing between idealistic and realist discourse, with domestic and international factors influencing the situation. First of all, Islamic Republic, did not aim to be isolated on international scene, being the protector of all the oppressed nations, Iran had a goal of avoiding domination. The Iran-Iraq war has left a negative opinion of the international organizations on Iran, when almost all the countries were giving support to Iraq. In the same time, Iran's idea of exporting revolution was terrifying for most of the Persian Gulf states, that was a threat to their sovereignty. It has also importance due to the fact that according to Iran's economic, security, cultural, and military foundations, history and geographic position in the Middle East, this country is seen as a constructive player in the Middle East. The instabilities in the region influence Iran, for its national interests it is required to support regional development. Due to these characteristics, the Islamic Republic of Iran can play a constructive role in the implementation of the Greater Middle East Plan, including political development, economic progress, etc. Iran's support for such plans requires granting it a proper regional role. Therefore, the author estimated Iran's position and role in the Middle East and also analyze the factors which promote the growing of it.

The changing of power in Iran in 1979 has changed its allies and therefore its position in the region. For example, at previous time Iran and Saudi Arabia were part of the Nixon doctrine and, thus, were providing its interests in the Middle East region. Appeared after the revolution, new slogan and principle of "Neither East nor West" illustrated the will of the country to find its own path, form its independent foreign policy and play a more constructive role in region and international scene. In this research the author underlined the main characteristics of Iran's foreign policy and place that Saudi Arabia and Syria occupy in it.

The Islamicization of the foreign policy of Iran shows that Imam Khomeini has a special place in explaining the principles of foreign policy. What matters is that Islam became a paradigm in foreign policy, and Iran's foreign policy became Islamized. The main point for Imam were: independence, the export of revolution, the unification of the Islamic Ummah, respect for rights Mutual, negation of oppression, good and peaceful relations with others, defending Islam and Muslims, principle of Neither East nor West, expansion of relations on the basis of Islamic and humanitarian principles and assistance to liberation movements. The principles of foreign policy designed by Imam Khomeini can be considered as one of the official sources of decision making in the policy of the Islamic Republic of Iran. In such a way that even the new leader of the Islamic Revolution has repeatedly stated that the general line in the policy of the Islamic Republic of Iran is the same as the one that Imam Khomeini has described. The same chapter also focuses on the priorities of Iran's foreign policy in the Middle East during the Bazargan and Mousavi governments. The Bazargan's government pursued a pragmatic and realistic discourse, while Mousavi's government was the value-centered one. In the end there is an analysis of the Iran-Iraq war and the role of Saudi Arabia in it, its financial and logistical support to Iraq. Syria on the contrary, was supporting Iran and became its ally, which responds to Iran's national interests and the development of the Hezbollah organization, its opposition to Israel.

After the 1989, pragmatism was the main policy of Iran. Rafsanjani government is known as the construction government. In this period of time there were the war-related issues, declining domestic production, hostility of Western countries, the collapse of the Soviet Union, the invasion of Iraq to Kuwait, the presence of the United States in the Persian Gulf. All of the mentioned caused the agents of the Islamic Republic of Iran to choose a realistic approach. But in spite of all the attempts by Khatami's government to change the attitude, after the September 11, 2001 Iran was named a part of the axis of evil, there was a presence of the United States in Afghanistan, their invasion in Iraq in 2003, the provocation of the Gulf states against Iran's nuclear program, etc. The foreign policy during the eight years of the Ahmadinejad government had the same base as the early ideals of the revolution, such as defending Palestine and the destruction of Israel. The slogan of Neither East nor West was brought back. This critical and aggressive approach has led to the security of Iran's position in the region and has led to a change in the discourse towards moderation (the government of Rouhani). With the arrival of Hassan Rouhani, who has concluded a nuclear deal with the group 5+1 after 12 years the main goal of his government is to maintain it and engage in economic activity. Then, in the last chapter, there is an analyze of the relations between Iran and Syria before and after the Arab Spring in the Middle East. Syria has common views with Iran, such as anti-imperialism, anti-Americanism and anti-Israeli approaches, support for Hezbollah and Hamas, the alliance of resistance against the influence of the United States and its allies in the region. The beginning of the Syrian crisis in the late 2010s was in the same time as the Arab Spring. But many researchers do not consider it to be a part of the Arab uprisings. They also assume that saving the Bashar al-Assad regime has strategic importance for Iran as an ally in the region. The four-member coalition (including Russia, Iran, Iraq and Syria) was formed against the United States-led anti-ISIL coalition, with many regional and international consequences. As can be seen in the third chapter, it can be concluded that Iran's foreign policy on the Syrian crisis is based on the following axes: stopping of violence in Syria, lack of political and military intervention of foreigners, and preservation of the state of Bashar al-Assad, as well as need for a reform. Iran, as well as Russia consider that only the Syrian people may choose their fate. Therefore, referring to people's votes to determine the future of the country is necessary. It can be concluded that Iran, both before and after the Arab Spring, has a special supporting role for the Syrian government with its realistic view. At the end of the chapter, which deals with Iran's relations with Saudi Arabia in the Middle East crisis region and the creation of a New Middle East, there is a study from the perspective of instrumental sectarianism, which, being as one of the components of regional order. The Iranian support for Syrian regime is explained not only by the religious proximity of Shiites and Alawites, but also by the strategic reasons that go back to 1979-1980. The secularized regime of Hafez al-Assad was the only Arab country, which supported Iran in its struggle against Iraq. Later this have led to a creation of Hezbollah, which put its belonging to Islam (and not to Shi'ism) in order to become an uncompromising actor of the Arab-Israeli conflict. Therefore, Syria has a strategic importance for the Islamic Republic. The dynamic of Iran-Syria relations throughout the post-revolutionary period starting with the Iran-Iraq war and after is shown by the author.

The 2010 Arab uprisings on the one hand exacerbated the power struggles in the Middle East, and on the other hand, led the governments of the region to become more instrumental in sectarianism. Therefore, the author examined Iran-Syria and Iran-Saudi Arabia relations before and after the Arab spring. In the process of sectarianism in the Middle East, powerful states use different strategies. Saudi Arabia, which plays a key role in Sunni sectarianism, has introduced the Shiites as an atheist minority and emphasized the role of Iran as a non-Arab actor in the Arab world seeking to exploit the vast majority of the Sunni world against Iran. On the contrary, Iran's desire is to rebuild the resistance of Muslims against the United States and Israel and their regional partners (led by Saudi Arabia). The Islamic Republic of Iran relies on the mobilization of the transnational network of Shiite minorities. It can be concluded that Iran and Saudi Arabia, with their sectarian views, tend to expand their influence. Also, with this sectarian view from Iran and Saudi Arabia, the hope for peace in the Middle East region cannot be imagined in the near future.

Sources of the research

Legislative documents

In English:

1. Iran (Iran Republic of)'s Constitution of 1979 with Amendments trough 1989. [electronic source]. Available at: https://www.constituteproject.org/constitution/Iran_1989.pdf?lang=en

2. Limits in the seas. Continental shelf boundary: Iran-Saudi Arabia // U.S. Department of State. [electronic source]. Available at: https://www.state.gov/documents/organization/61606.pdf

In Persian:

3. Website containing the laws of the Islamic Republic of Iran. [electronic source]. Available at: http://lawiran.ir/

Documents of international organizations

In English:

4. Chapter VIII. Considerations of questions under the council's responsibility for the maintenance of international peace and security [electronic source]. Available at: http://www.un.org/ar/sc/repertoire/85-88/85-88_08.pdf

5. Joint Comprehensive Plan of Action implementation and verification and monitoring in the Islamic Republic of Iran in light of United Nations Security Council Resolution 2231 (2015) // IAEA [electronic source]. Available at: https://www.iaea.org/sites/default/files/gov-2015-72-derestricted.pdf

Publicistic documents

In English:

6.   Ayatollah Khamenei's Opinion on Unity [electronic source]. Available at: http://english.khamenei.ir/Opinions/tunity

7.   Islamic Republic of Iran, Permanent Mission to the United Nations, Address by H.E. Doctor Mahmoud Ahmadinejad President of the Islamic Republic of Iran before the Sixty-Second Session of the United Nations General Assembly // United Nations, 2007 [electronic source]. Available at: http://www.un.org/webcast/ga/62/2007/pdfs/iran-eng.pdf

8.   Khomeini: "We Shall Confront the World with Our Ideology" // Radio Iran, 1980. [electronic source]. Available at http://www.merip.org/mer/mer88/khomeini-we-shall-confront-world-our-ideology

9.   Velayati A. A. First Speech // Foreign Policy Magazine No. 1. 1986.

What are statuses and duties of the "Expediency Council" in the Iranian system? 2017. [electronic source]. Available at: http://english.khamenei.ir/news/5072/What-are-statuses-and-duties-of-the-Expediency-Council-in-the

In Persian:

10. Ahmadi A. Ahmadinejad is searching for the resolving of the nuclear deal through the conversation with Europe, 2013. [electronic source]. Available at:

http://donya-e-eqtesad.com

11.   Imam Khomeini speaking abt the Iran Iraq war – Persian. [electronic source]. Available at: https://www.shiatv.net/video/bb322f89a226bd2c5d41

Statistics

In English:

12.   Annual report // Organization of the Petroleum Exporting Countries, 2016. [electronic source].   Available   at: http://www.opec.org/opec_web/static_files_project/media/downloads/publications/AR%202016.pdf

13.   BP Statistical Review of World Energy. [electronic source]. Available at: http://www.bp.com

14.   CIA The World Factbook. [electronic source]. Available at: https://www.cia.gov

15. U.S. Energy Information Administration. [electronic source]. Available at: https://www.eia.gov

16. U.S. Geological Survey Minerals Yearbook. [electronic source]. Available at: https://minerals.usgs.gov

In Persian:

17. Iran: Statistics - Pars Times [electronic source]. Available at: http://www.parstimes.com/statistics/

18. Statistic Research and Training Center [electronic source]. Available at: http://srtc.ac.ir/fa

Historical sources

In English:

19. 400 die as Iranian marchers battle Saudi police in Mecca; embassies smashed in Teheran // The New York Times, 1987. [electronic source]. Available at: http://www.nytimes.com/1987/08/02/world/400-die-iranian-marchers-battle-saudi-police-mecca-embassies-smashed-teheran.html?pagewanted=all

20. Abu H. Firas. Iran and the Arab Revolutions: positions and Repercussions //Arab Center for Research and Policy Studies. 2011. [electronic source]. Available at: http://english.dohainstitute.org/file/get9a915419-721c-45ab-aa11-1cbac8dbaac3.pdf

21. Adib-Moghaddam A. Iran and the world after Rouhani // University of London, 2017-2018. [electronic source]. Available at: http://www.ide.go.jp/library/Japanese/Publish/Periodicals/Me_review/pdf/201709_01.pdf

22. Afrasiabi K. L. After Khomeini: New Directions in Iran's Foreign Policy // Westview Press. Boulder CO. 1994.

23. Aitani A.M.,, Halim S.H. Downstream in the Persian Gulf-2 //King Fahd University of Petroleum & Minerals. Oil and Gaz Journal. 1997. [electronic source]. Available at: https://www.researchgate.net/profile/Abdullah_Aitani/publication/258258689_DOWNSTREAM

24. Al-Lihaibi M.A. An analysis of the Iran-Iraq war: military strategy and political objectives // Research report. Air war college. Air university release; distribution United States air force,

Maxwell air force base, Alabama, 1989. [electronic source]. Available at: http://www.dtic.mil/dtic/tr/fulltext/u2/a217255.pdf

25. Althunayyan H. The U.S.-Saudi relations in the Trump era // Aljazeera Media Network. 2017. [electronic source]. Available at: http://www.aljazeera.com/indepth/opinion/2017/05/saudi-relations-trump-era-170518084540044.html

26. An EU Strategy for Relations with Iran After the Nuclear Deal, 2016. Arab Petroleum Exporting Countries to Meet In Libya // The North Africa Post, 2013. [electronic source]. Available at: http://northafricapost.com/2960-arab-petroleum-exporting-countries-to-meet-in-libya.html

27. Arnson C., Esfandiary H., Strubits A. Iran in Latin America. Threat of "Axes of Annoyance"? // Woodrow Wilson Center Reports, 2007. [electronic source]. Available at: https://www.wilsoncenter.org/sites/default/files/Iran_in_LA.pd

28. Asisian N. Russia & Iran: Strategic Alliance or Marriage of Convenience // Small Wars Journal, 2013.

29. Ayatollah Khamenei's Opinion on Unity [electronic source]. Available at: http://english.khamenei.ir/Opinions/tunity

30. Banco A., E. Brexit Impact: UK Could Drop Sanctions to Trade with Iran // International Business Times. 2016 [electronic source]. Available at: http://www.ibtimes.com/brexit-impact-uk-could-drop-sanctions-trade-iran-.172883

31. Barabandi B., Thompsona T.J. Friend of my Father: Iran's Manipulation of Bashar al-Assad // Atlantic Council, 2014. [electronic source]. Available at: http://www.atlanticcouncil.org/blogs/menasource/a-friend-of-my-father-iran-s-manipulation-of-bashar-al-assad

32. Barry J., Arbarzadeh S. State identity in Iranian foreign policy // British Journal of Middle Eastern Studies, 2016. [electronic source]. Available at: http://www.tandfonline.com/doi/abs/10.1080/13530194.2016.1159541?src=recsys&journalCode=cbjm20

33. Bastani H. How Powerful is Rouhani in the Islamic Republic? // Middle East and North Africa Programme, 2004. [electronic source]. Available at:

34. Bazargan's interview with Oriana Fallaci // The New Yorker, 1979.

35. Borujerdi A.H. Development of Arab-Iranian relations // Publishing house of Ministry of Foreign Affairs, Tehran. 2001, p. 145.

36. Branckaert J. Musings of a Eurasian future // Journal of Eurasian Affairs, 2013. [electronic source]. Available at: http://www.eurasianaffairs.net/musings-of-a-eurasian-future/

37.   Byman D. Strange Bedfellows. What's behind the enduring alliance between Syria and Iran?, 2006.   [electronic   source].   Available   at: http://www.slate.com/articles/news_and_politics/foreigners/2006/07/strange_bedfellows.html

38.   Chapter V Syria and Her Non-Arab Neighbours [electronic source]. Available at: http://shodhganga.inflibnet.ac.in/bitstream/10603/17356/10/10_chapter%205.pdf

39.   Clawson P., Eisenstadt M., Kanovsky E., Menashri D. Iran under Khatami: a political, economic, and military assessment // The Washington Institute for Near East Policy, 1998.

40.   Clemente J. U.S. Oil Production Will Continue To Grow, 2016. [electronic source]. Available   at: https://www.forbes.com/sites/judeclemente/2016/08/09/u-s-oil-production-will-continue-to-grow/#2235c0442677

41.   Cross-Border Oil and Gas Pipelines: Problems and Prospects // Joint UNDP/World Bank Energy Sector Management Assistance Programme (ESMAP), 2003. [electronic source]. Available at: http://siteresources.worldbank.org/INTOGMC/Resources/crossborderoilandgaspipelines.pdf

42.   Daniels O., Brown C. China's Energy Security Achilles Heel: Middle Eastern Oil // The Diplomat, 2015. [electronic source]. Available at: https://thediplomat.com/2015/09/chinas-energy-security-achilles-heel-middle-eastern-oil/

43.   Darwisha A. Islam in foreign policy // Cambridge university press, 1983.

44.   Diaz Sanz M. The Geopolitical Challenge of the Non-Aligned: Iran 2012-2015 // E-International Relations, 2012. [electronic source]. Available at: http://www.e-ir.info/2012/09/26/the-geopolitical-challenge-of-the-non-aligned-iran-2012-2015/

45.   Djalili M.R. Iran-Iraq: radioscopie dune guerre ambigue, (Iran-Iraq: radioscopy of an ambiguous war) // Politique Internationale, 1983.

46.   Donald Trump: we should milk the fat Saudi Arabia as much as possible, and when the wealthy sheikhs become useless we should abandon the Middle-East // The World Observer. 2011. [electronic source]. Available at: https://www.theworldobserver.com.au/index.php/world-news-2/americas/10268

47.   El-Labbad M. Egypt:A Regional Reference in the Middle East. In Henner Furtig(ed).Regional Powers in the Middle East: New Constellations after the Arab Revolts // New York: Palgrave. 2014.

48.   Esfahani A.S. Cultural Globalization and Foreign Policy Strategies of the Islamic Republic of Iran (Case Study; the Seventh and the Ninth Governments) // Published by Canadian Center of Science   and   Education,   2017.   [electronic   source].   Available   at: https://www.google.ru/url?sa=t&rct=j&q=&esrc=s&source=web&cd=1&ved=0ahUKEwjwka3g

49.   Esfandiary D., Tabatabai A. Yemen: an Opportunity for Iran-Saudi Dialogue? //The Washington Quarterly. Volume 39, Issue 2, 2016.

50.   Esposito J. The Iranian revolution and its global reflection, translation by Doctor Shanechi M.M. Article issuing the Iranian revolution: politics, objectives and instruments, Ramezani R.K. // Tehran: Center for the recognition of Islam and Iran, 2003.

51.   Etaat J. Geopolitical Characteristics of the Middle East // Series on Middle East Studies, 1996.

52.   Filipkova L., Hesova Z., Karasek T., Kubikova N., Kuzvart J., Zahora J. NATO and the Arab Spring: challenge to cooperation,Opportunity for Action? // Association for International Affairs. 2012. [electronic source]. Available at: https://www.amo.cz/wp-content/uploads/2015/11/pp-2012-01.pdf

53.   Freilich C. The Middle East after the Iran Nuclear Deal // Council Foreign Relations. 2015. [electronic source]. Available at: https://www.cfr.org/expert-roundup/middle-east-after-iran-nuclear-deal

54.   Fullton W. Ali Akbar Velayati: A Window into the Foreign Policy of Iran's Supreme Leader // Critical threats, 2011. [electronic source]. Available at https://www.criticalthreats.org/analysis/ali-akbar-velayati-a-window-into-the-foreign-policy-of-irans-supreme-leader

55.   Gause G. Beyond Sectarianism: The New Middle East Cold War // Brookings Doha Center. 2014 [electronic source]. Available at: https://www.brooking.edu/wp-content/uploads/2016/06/English-PDF-1.pdf

56.   Gause G. Is Saudi Arabia really counter-revolutionary? // The Middle East channel // Foreign policy. 2011 [electronic source]. Available at: http://foreignpolicy.com/2011/08/09/is-saudi-arabia-really-counter-revolutionary/

57.   Gause G. The Future of U.S – Saudi Relations: The Kingdom and the Power // Foreign Affairs. Volume 95, Issue 4. 2015.

58.   Goldsmith L. (2011), Syria's Alawites and the Politics of sectarian Insecurity: a Khaldunian Perspective // Middle Eastern Studies. University of Otago. Volume 3, Pages 33-60 [electronic source].   Available   at: https://www.researchgate.net/publication/281230449_Syria%27s_Alawites_and_the_Politics_of_Sectarian_Insecurity_A_Khaldunian_Perspective

59.   Goodarzi J. Iran and Syria at the Crossroads: The Fall of the Tehran-Damascus Axis? // International Relations Department, Webster University, Geneva, Wilson Center, 2013. [electronic source].   Available   at:

https://www.wilsoncenter.org/sites/default/files/iran_syria_crossroads_fall_tehran_damascus_axis.pdf

60.   Goodarzi J.M. The formative years of the Syrian-Iran alliance: power politics in the Middle East 1979-1989 [electronic source]. Available at: http://etheses.lse.ac.uk/1651/1/U162952.pdf

61.   Graham E. Fuller. The center of the universe: The geopolitics of Iran (Rand Corporation Research Study) // Orbis, 1992.

62.   Hafez al-Assad // The Guardian, 2000. [electronic source]. Available at: https://www.theguardian.com/theguardian/2000/jun/15/guardianweekly.guardianweekly1

63.   Hafezi P., Sedarat F. Ahmadinejad says Holocaust a lie, Israel has no future, 2009. [electronic source]. Available at: http://www.reuters.com/article/us-iran/ahmadinejad-says-holocaust-a-lie-israel-has-no-future-idUSTRE58H17S20090918

64.   Haghighat S. S. Confluence Theory & Religious Leadership Theory // Mofid University, Qom, Iran, 2017. [electronic source]. Available at: http://www.mofidu.ac.ir/_DouranPortal/Documents/C.V._ENGLISH_%20_2__20170730_080041.pdf

65.   Hammond J.R. Full Text of President Ahmadinejad's Remarks at U.N. Conference on Racism // Foreign Policy Journal, 2009. [electronic source]. Available at: https://www.foreignpolicyjournal.com/2009/04/21/full-text-of-president-ahmadinejads-remarks-at-un-conference-on-racism/

66.   Henrikson A.K. What can public diplomacy achieve? Discussion Papers in Diplomacy // Netherland Institute of International relations "Clingendael", 2006. [electronic source]. Available at: https://www.diplomatie.gouv.fr/IMG/pdf/publicdiplo.pdf Ibid.

67.   Herzig, E. Islam, Transnationalism and Sub-regionalism in Cis countries, translated by Ejtehadi, A. // Quarterly Journal of Central Asia and the Caucasus, 2000.

68.   Hinnebusch R. A. The sectarian revolution in the Middle East // Aloysius. In: R/Evolutions: Global Trends & Regional Issues, 2016.

69.   Hinnebusch R. A. The sectarianization of the Middle East: Transnational identity wars and competitive interference. Project on Middle East political science (POMEPS) // University of St. Andrews. June 8–9, 2016. [electronic source]. Available at: https://pomeps.org/wp-content/uploads/2016/09/POMEPS-studies-21-transnational_Web-REV.pdf

70.   Hinnebusch R. The Arab Uprisings and the MENA Regional States System // Uluslararasi ilishikler. Volume 11, Issue 42, 2014.

71.   Holland J. The First Iraq War Was Also Sold to the Public Based on a Pack of Lies // Moyers & company, 2014. [electronic source]. Available at: http://billmoyers.com/2014/06/27/the-first-iraq-war-was-also-sold-to-the-public-based-on-a-pack-of-lies/

72.   HSU S. China's Relations With Iran: A Threat to the West? // The Diplomat. 2016 [electronic source]. Available at: http://thediplomat.com/2016/01/chinas-relations-withiran-a-threat-to-the-west/

http://thedailyjournalist.com/the-strategist/regionalimplications-of-the-jcpoa/

http://www.nytimes.com/1987/08/02/world/400-die-iranian-marchers-battle-saudi-police-mecca-embassies-smashed-teheran.html?pagewanted=all

https://www.chathamhouse.org/sites/files/chathamhouse/field/field_document/20141124RouhaniislamicRepublicBastani.pdf

73.   Hussein J. Agha and Ahmad. Syria and Iran (rivalry and cooperation) // London Wellington House, 1995.

74.   Impact on foreign policy // RAND [electronic source]. Available at: https://www.rand.org/content/dam/rand/pubs/monograph_reports/MR1320/MR1320.ch6.pdf

75.   International Energy Outlook // Energy Information Administration Office of Integrated Analysis and Forecasting U.S. Department of Energy Washington, 2007. [electronic source]. Available at: http://test.ricerchetrasporti.it/wp-content/uploads/downloads/file_1235.pdf

76.   Invasion Revisited: How Saudi Arabia backed Saddam's war on Iran? // The Iran Project, 2016. [electronic source]. Available at: http://theiranproject.com/blog/2016/09/28/invasion-revisited-saudi-arabia-backed-saddams-war-iran/

77.   Invasion Revisited: How Saudi Arabia Backed Saddam's War on Iran? //Alwaght, 2016. [electronic source]. Available at: http://alwaght.com/en/News/68927/Invasion-Revisited-How-Saudi-Arabia-Backed-Saddam%E2%80%99s-War-on-Iran?

78.   Iran, Hizbullah, Hamas and the global Jihad. A new conflict paradigm for the West // Jerusalem Center for Public Affairs, 2007. [electronic source]. Available at: http://jcpa.org/wp-content/uploads/2012/08/iran-hizbullah-hamas.pdf

79.   Iran, the United States and a Political Seesaw // The New York Times, 2012.

80.   Iran. Other Relevant Middle East Conflicts // Understanding the Iran-Contra Affairs [electronic source]. Available at: https://www.brown.edu/Research/Understanding_the_Iran_Contra_Affair/i-otherconflicts.php

81.   Iran-Iraq war [electronic source]. Available at: https://www.saylor.org/site/wp-content/uploads/2011/08/HIST351-11.1.4-Iran-Iraq-War.pdf

82. Iran-Iraq war timeline [electronic source]. Available at: https://www.wilsoncenter.org/sites/default/files/Iran-IraqWar_Part1_0.pdf

83. Iran's Politics and Foreign Policy // Chatham House, 2016. [electronic source]. Available at: https://www.chathamhouse.org/event/irans-politics-and-foreign-policy

84. Jones P. Towards a regional security regime for the Middle East // Stockholm International Peace Research Institute (SIPRI), 1998. [electronic source]. Available at: https://www.files.ethz.ch/isn/96416/1998_12_SIPRI98Jones.pdf

85. Kalin I. Sectarianism: A Recipe for Disaster for Sunnis and Shiites. 2014. [electronic source]. Available at: https://www.dailysabah.com/columns/ibrahim-kalin/2014/06/17/sectarianism-a-recipe-for-disaster-for-sunnis-and-shiites

86. Kamali H.R. Iran and Saudi Arabia: Past and Future // Iran Review, 2014. [electronic source]. Available at: http://www.iranreview.org/content/Documents/Iran-and-Saudi-Arabia-Past-and-Future.htm

87. Kar M. The future of Iran: judicial reform. Who are the judges in the Islamic Republic of Iran // Legatum Institute. [electronic source]. Available at: https://www.li.com/docs/default-source/future-of-iran/2012-future-of-iran-by-mehrangiz-kar-who-are-the-judges-in-the-islamic-republic-of-iran.pdf?sfvrsn=2

88. Karami A. Saudi Prince's endorsement of MEK angers Iranian officials // AL-Monitor. 2016 [electronic source]. Available at: http://www.al-monitor.com/pulse/originals/2016/07/iran-mek-mojahedin-saudi-turki-bin-faisal.html

89. Karl E. Meyer. Editorial Notebook; How the Middle East Was Invented // The New York Times. 1991. [electronic source]. Available at: http://www.nytimes.com/1991/03/13/opinion/editorial-notebook-how-the-middle-east-was-invented.html

90. Katzman K. Iran: U.S. Concerns and Policy Responses // Congressional Research Sources, 2012. [electronic source]. Available at: https://www.hsdl.org/?view&did=704460

91. Katzman K. Iran's foreign policy // Congressional Research Service, 2016 [electronic source]. Available at: https://www.hsdl.org/?view&did=793975.

92. Kazemzadeh M. Foreign policy decision making in Iran and the nuclear program // Taylor&Francis online, 2017. [electronic source]. Available at: http://www.tandfonline.com/doi/abs/10.1080/01495933.2017.1338478?needAccess=true&journalCode=ucst20

93.   Kessler M.N., Irani G., Gubser P., Norton A. R., Chas. W., Freeman Jr. Lebanon and Syria: Internal and Regional Dimensions // Middle East Policy Council, 2001. [electronic source]. Available at: http://www.mepc.org/journal/lebanon-and-syria-internal-and-regional-dimensions

94.   Khaddour H. How regional security concerns uniquely constrain governance in Northeastern Syria // Carnegie Middle East Center, 2017. [electronic source]. Available at: http://carnegieendowment.org/files/CMEC_66_Khaddour_Jazira_FInal_Web.pdf

95.   Khalid A. Iran calls on Syrian President to consider protesters demands // Independent. 2011. [electronic source]. Available at: http://www.independent.co.uk/news/world/middle-east/iran-calls-on-syrian-president-to-consider-protesters-demands-2345536.html

96.   Khoury N.A. The Arab Cold War Revisited: The Regional Impact of the Arab Uprising // Middle East Policy 20 (2): 2013.

97.   Kiasat H., Afshooni M. Iran's diplomatic behavior from the Revolution until the end of the war // Islamic Azad University, 2016. [electronic source]. Available at: http://docsdrive.com/pdfs/medwelljournals/sscience/2016/4224-4230.pdf

98.   Koch C. Constructing a viable EU-GCC partnership // Gulf Research Center Foundation. 2014 [electronic source]. Available at: http://eprints.lse.ac.uk/55282/1/Constructing-aviable-U-GCC-relationship.pdf(accessed

99.   Kofner J. 400 die as Iranian marchers battle Saudi police in Mecca; embassies smashed in Teheran // The New York Times, 1987. [electronic source]. Available at:

100.   Kurzman C. The Arab Spring: Ideals of the Iranian Green Movement, Methods of the Iranian Revolution // International Journal of Middle East Studies. Volume 44, Issue 1, 2012.

101.   Lasdayr D., Blake J. H. The geopolitics of the Middle East and North Africa, translated by Mirheydar D., (Mohajerani) // Tehran. The office of political and international studies. 1992.

102.   Lasensky S. Special report. Iraq and its neighbors, 2006. [electronic source]. Available at: http://dspace.africaportal.org/jspui/bitstream/123456789/15081/1/Jordan%20and%20Iraq%20Between%20Cooperation%20and%20Crisis.pdf?1

103.   Leader Meets with Government Officials, 2013. [electronic source]. Available at: http://english.khamenei.ir/news/1807/Leader-Meets-with-Government-Officials

104.   Leeden M., Levis W. Debacle: The American Fallure in Iran // New York: Knopf, 1980.

105.   Levitt M. Iran's Support for Terrorism under the JCPOA // Washington Institute. 2016 [electronic source]. Available at: http://www.washingtoninstitute.org/policyanalysis/view/irans-support-for-terrorism-under-the-jcpoa

106. Lim K. National Security Decision-Making in Iran // Taylor & Francis. 2015. [electronic source]. Available at: http://www.tandfonline.com/doi/abs/10.1080/01495933.2015.1017347

107. Mabon S. The Battle for Bahrain: Iranian-Saudi Rivalry // East Policy. Volume 19, Issue 2, 2012.

108. Macfarquhar N. Hafez al-Assad, Who Turned Syria Into a Power in the Middle East, Dies at 69 // The New York Times, 2010. [electronic source]. Available at: http://www.nytimes.com/2000/06/11/world/hafez-al-assad-who-turned-syria-into-a-power-in-the-middle-east-dies-at-69.html

109. Makinen H. The future of natural gas as the European Union's energy source – risks and possibilities // Electronic Publications of Pan-European Institute, 2010. [electronic source]. Available at: https://www.utu.fi/fi/yksikot/tse/yksikot/PEI/raportit-ja-tietopaketit/Documents/M%C3%A4kinen_final.pdf

110. Maltzahn N. V. The Syria-Iran Axis: Cultural Diplomacy and International Relations in the Middle East // Library of Modern Middle East Studies // I.B.Tauris & Co Ltd. 2015.

111. Matthiesen T. Transnational Identities after the Arab Uprising, in Luigi Narbone and Martin Lestra(eds), The Gulf Monarchies beyond the Arab spring: changes and challenges // Florence : European University Institute. 2015.

112. Mir-Khalili S.J. Imam Khomeini's Viewpoints on Iranian Foreign Policy// Iran Review, 2008.

113. Mofid K. The cost of the Iran-Iraq war has been estimated at $1.097 billion. The Economic Consequences of the Gulf War // New York: Routlefge, 1990.

114. Mohseni P. Iran and the Arab World after the Nuclear Deal: Rivalry and Engagement in a New Era // Belfer Center for Science and International Affairs, 2015.

115. Mossad A. M. Nouvelle orientation de la deuxieme republique iranienne: priorites-instrument-contraintes in Crise du golfe et ordre politique au Moyen- Orient (The crisis of Gulf and the Middle Eastern political order), edited by Micheal Camau, A.E. Hilal Dessouki, and J. C. Vatin // Paris: CNRS, 1993.

116. Narbone L., Lestra M. The Gulf Monarchies beyond the Arab spring: changes and challenges // Florence : European University Institute, 2015 [electronic source]. Available at: http://cadmus.eui.eu/handle/1814/37734

117. Nazemroaya M.D. Plans for Redrawing the Middle East: The Project for a "New Middle East" //GlobalResearch. 2016. [electronic source]. Available at:

https://www.globalresearch.ca/plans-for-redrawing-the-middle-east-the-project-for-a-new-middle-east/3882

118. Nia M. M. Title: A Holistic Constructivist Approach to Iran's Foreign Policy // International Journal of business and social science, 2011. [electronic source]. Available at: http://ijbssnet.com/journals/Vol._2_No._4;_March_2011/31.pdf

119. O'Bagy E. The free Syrian Army // Institute for the Study of War. 2013 [electronic source]. Available at: http://www.understandingwar.org/sites/default/files/The-Free-Syrian Army-24MAR.pdf

120. Parsi R. Iran: a revolutionary republic in transition // Challiot Papers, 2012. [electronic source]. Available at: https://www.iss.europa.eu/sites/default/files/EUISSFiles/cp128-Iran_A_revolutionary_republic_in_transition_0.pdf

121. Peres S., Naor A. The New Middle East // Henry Holt & Co; 1 edition. 1993.

122. Phillips J. The Dangerous Regional Implications of the Iran Nuclear Agreement // Heritage. 2015. [electronic source]. Available at: http://www.org/research/reports/2016/05/the-dangerous-regional-implications of-the- iran-nuclear-agreement.

123. Polk W.R. Understanding Syria: From Pre-Civil War to Post-Assad // The Atlantic, 2013. [electronic source]. Available at: https://www.theatlantic.com/international/archive/2013/12/understanding-syria-from-pre-civil-war-to-post-assad/281989/

124. Pollack K. M. Containing Iran // The Iran Primer. United States Institute of Peace, 2010.

125. Pollack, K. M. U.S. Policy toward the Middle East after the Iranian Nuclear Agreement // Brookings. [electronic source]. Available at: https://www.brookings.edu/testimonies/u-s-policy-toward-the-middle-eastafter-the -iranian-nuclear-agreement/

126. President Carter and the Role of Intelligence in the Camp David Accords // Jimmy Carter Presidential Library, 2013. [electronic source]. Available at: https://www.cia.gov/library/publications/international-relations/president-carter-and-the-camp-david-accords/Carter_CampDavid_Pub.pdf

127. Rivera J. Iran's Involvement in Bahrain // Small Wall War Journal. 2012. [electronic source]. Available at: http://smallwarsjournal.com/jrnl/iran%E2%80%99s-involvement-in-bahrain

128. Rodriquez C. The Iraqi Disarmament Crisis: What Lessons Can Be Learned? // E-International relations student, 2017. [electronic source]. Available at: http://www.e-ir.info/2017/10/02/the-iraqi-disarmament-crisis-what-lessons-can-be-learned/

129. Ruff A. Growing Russia-Iran Military Relations: An Illusion? //Foreign Policy News. 2016 [electronic source]. Available at: http://f.org/2016/09/02/growing-russia-iranmilitary-relations-illusion/

130. Sadeghi B., Tabatabai S. M. Metaphor Analysis and Discursive Cycle of Iran's Foreign Policy: "Justice" through the lenses of US-IRAN Presidents // Cumhuriyet University Faculty of Science Science Journal, 2015. [electronic source]. Available at: http://dergi.cumhuriyet.edu.tr/cumuscij/article/viewFile/5000121835/5000114490

131. Salloukh B. Syria and Lebanon: A Brotherhood Transformed [electronic source]. Available at: http://www.merip.org/mer/mer236/syria-lebanon-brotherhood-transformed

132. Samii W. A Stable Structure on Shifting Sands: Assessing the Hizbullah-Iran-Syria Relationship // Middle East Institute. [electronic source]. Available at: http://www.sino-west.org/sjtu/Stable.pdf

133. Sarmadi H., Badri M. The Effect of Hashemi Rafsanjani's Technocrat Government and changing of foreign policy of Iran from power to pragmatism // Academia Journal of Educational Research, 2017. [electronic source]. Available at: https://www.academiapublishing.org/journals/ajer/pdf/2017/Feb/Sarmadi%20and%20Badri.pdf

134. Schmierer R.J, Jeffrey J. F., Nader A., Nazer F. The Saudi-Iranian Rivalry and the Obama Doctrine // Middle East Policy Council, 2016. [electronic source]. Available at: http://www.mepc.org/saudi-iranian-rivalry-and-obama-doctrine-0

135. Seale P. Assad. The struggle for the Middle East // London: I.B. Taurus, 1988.

136. Segal D. The Iran-Iraq War: A Military Analysis // Foreign Affairs, 1998. [electronic source]. Available at: https://www.foreignaffairs.com/articles/iran/1988-06-01/iran-iraq-war-military-analysis

137. Sela A. The Changing Focus of the Arab State System // Middle East Review, 1988.

138. Shahram Chubin and Charl, s Tripp. Iran and Iraq at war // London: I.B, Tauris, 1988.

139. Shaw M. Sociological approaches to international relations // University of Sussex, UK, 2009.

140. Sheikh Attar A. The roots of political behavior in Central Asia and Caucasus // Tehran: Institute for political and international studies Press. 1994.

141. Shokooee, H. The term and concept of the Middle East: the Failure of a Geographical Term, Tabriz // University Journal of the Faculty of Literature and Humanities. 1968.

142. Sick G. Regional Implications of the JCPOA // The Daily Journalist. 2016. [electronic source]. Available at: http://thedailyjournalist.com/the-strategist/regionalimplications-of-the-jcpoa/

143.   Significant Terrorist Incidents, 1961-2003: A Brief Chronology // U.S. Department of State archives. [electronic source]. Available at: https://2001-2009.state.gov/r/pa/ho/pubs/fs/5902.htm

144.   Singh P. Conceptual understanding of geopolitics with special reference to Indian Ocean // International Journal of Applied Research, 2015. [electronic source]. Available at: http://www.allresearchjournal.com/archives/2015/vol1issue6/PartF/1-5-109.1.pdf

145.   Smith W. Our Defense is a Holy Defense! - The Iran-Iraq War and its Legacy in Contemporary Iranian Factional Politics // Journal of Georgetown University-Qatar. Middle Eastern Studies Students Association, 2015. [electronic source]. Available at: http://www.qscience.com/doi/pdf/10.5339/messa.2015.3

146.   Soltani N. A. Foreign policy of Syria in crisis and internal war (1975-1990) // Quarterly military reviews, 1995.

147.   Stewart S., Assessing Hezbollah Kidnapping Threats in Lebanon //Stratfor, 2013. [electronic source]. Available at: https://www.stratfor.com/weekly/assessing-hezbollah-kidnapping-threats-lebanon?topics=298

148.   Swenson E. What Happens When Islamists Take Power? The Case of Iran, 2005.

149.   Tabaar M. A. Factional politics in the Iran–Iraq war // Taylor & Francis, 2017. [electronic source]. Available at: http://www.tandfonline.com/doi/abs/10.1080/01402390.2017.1347873

150.   Tabrizi A.B., Pantiucci R. Understanding Iran's Role in the Syrian Conflict // Royal United Services Institute for Defence and Security Studies, 2016. [electronic source] Available at:https://rusi.org/sites/default/files/201608_op_understanding_irans_role_in_the_syrian_conflict_0.pdf

151.   Tarr D.G. Export Restraints on Russian Natural Gas and Raw Timber: What are the Economic Impacts? // CEPE Working Paper No. 74, 2010. [electronic source]. Available at: https://www.ethz.ch/content/dam/ethz/special-interest/mtec/cepe/cepe-dam/documents/research/cepe-wp/CEPE_WP74.pdf

152.   The 1973 Arab-Israeli War: Arab Policies, Strategies, and Campaigns // Global security, 1997.

153.   The 1979 "Oil Shock:" Legacy, Lessons, and Lasting Reverberations // The Middle East Institute, Washington, DC [electronic source]. Available at: http://www.la.utexas.edu/users/chenry/public_html/elephants/OilShock201979-Final.pdf

154.   The arming of Saudi Arabia, 1993. [electronic source]. Available at: http://s3.amazonaws.com/911timeline/1990s/frontline0121693.html

155. The Iran nuclear deal: full text, 2013. [electronic source]. Available at: http://edition.cnn.com/2013/11/24/world/meast/iran-deal-text/index.html

156. The Kings Of The Kingdom. King AbdulAziz bin AbdulRahman bin Faisal Al Saud (1876 – 1953) // Ministry of Commerce and Investment. [electronic source]. Available at: http://mci.gov.sa/en/AboutKingdom/Pages/KingdomKings.aspx

157. The Nuclear Deal is a Chance to Change Iran's Behavior // The National interest, 2016. [electronic source]. Available at: http://nationalinterest.org/feature/the-nuclear-deal-chance-change-irans-behavior-17250

158. Thiel T. After the Arab Spring power shift in Middle East?:Yemen's Arab Spring: from youth revolution to fragile political transition // LSE Research Online. London School of Economics and Political Science. 2012. [electronic source]. Available at: https://www.lse,ac.uk/IDEAS/publications/reports/pdf/SR011/FINAL_LSE_IDEAS_Yemen's Arab Spring_Thiel.pdf

159. Tierney J. The Iran Deal: One Year Later, the Facts Point to Success // Huffington Post. 2016 [electronic source]. Available at: https://www.huffingtonpost.com/john-tierney/the-iran-deal-one-year-la_b_10948878.html

160. Torabi N. JCPOA: Rouhani's true Worth and Implications for Businesses in Iran. 2016 [electronic source]. Available at: https://www.linkedin.com/pulse/jcpoa-iirouhanis-true-worth-implications-businesses-iran-nima-torabi

161. Ulrichsen K. C. The Uprising in Bahrain: Regional Dimensions and International Consequences, in Larbi Sadiki(ed) // Routledge Handbook of the Arab Spring: Rethinking Democratization // New York: Routledge Taylor & Francis Group. 2015.

162. Vaezi M. Geopolitics of crisis in Central Asia and Caucasus // Tehran: Institute for political and international studies Press, 2007.

163. Why did the U.S. support Saddam in the Iran-Iraq War, but fought against him in Kuwait? // Quora, 2016. [electronic source]. Available at: https://www.quora.com/Why-did-the-US-support-Saddam-in-the-Iran-Iraq-War-but-fought-against-him-in-Kuwait

164. Wilfarm F. Hanrieder. Foregn Policies and the International System: A Theoretical International // New York: General Learning Press, 1971.

165. Wilfram F. Hanrieder. Compatibility and Consensus: A Proposal for the Conceptual Linking of External and Internal Dimensions of Foreign Policy // American Political Science Review, 1965.

166. Yusgiantoro P. Petroleum will still be the major energy resource in the 21st century, 2004. [electronic source]. Available at: http://www.opec.org/opec_web/en/902.htm

167. Zarate J. C. The Implications of Sanctions Relief under the Iran Agreement // Center for Strategic and International Studies (CSIS). 2015. [electronic source]. Available at: https://csis-prod.s3.amazonaws.com/s3fs-public/legacy_files/files/attachments/ts150805_Zarate.pdf

In Persian:

168. Settlement of the nuclear deal. Second salute to Iran // Aftabnews.ir.,2015. [electronic source]. Available at:http://aftabnews.ir/fa/news/303023/

169. [electronic source]. Available at: http://www.etelaterooz.ir/fa/doc/news/2694/

170. (In English) [electronic source]. Available at: http://www.entekhab.ir/fa/news/125970 reign policy of Iran during the period of Hatami in the words of Zarif, 2014. [electronic source]. Available at: http://www.yjc.ir/fa/news/4813696

171. Firoozabadi D., Jalal S. Discourse Transformation in the Foreign Policy of the Islamic Republic of Iran // Tehran, Iran Institute, 2005.

172. Mohammad-Ali Hosseinzadeh, Governing discourses over government after revolution in Islamic Republic of Iran, Documentation Center of Islamic revolution.

173. Azghandi A. The foreign policy of the Islamic Republic of Iran // Tehran: Qumis publishing, 2002.

174. The Imposed war and Oil - second part: the role of oil in the continuation of the Holy Defense // The site of the holy defense science and education research center [electronic source]. Available at: http://www.dsrc.ir/View/article.aspx?id=713

175. Lotfollahzadegan A. The Iran-Iraq War, Crossing the Border // Tehran: Center for War Studies and Research, 2002.

176. Ardebili H. K. Return to Neither West nor East policy // Diplomatic Citizen, 1996.

177. Maleki A. Foreign Policy of Iran // Italian Marco Polo Magazine. Naples, Institute of International Relations, Italy. 1997.

178. Mohammadi M. Foreign Policy of the Islamic Republic of Iran. Principles and Issues of Tehran // Publishing House of Dastgostar. 1998.

179. Moghattar H. Discussions on International Politics and Foreign Policy // Tehran, Faculty of Political and Social Sciences. 1979.

180. Khoshghat M.H., Foreign Policy Decision-making Analysis // Tehran, Publishing institute, Ministry of Foreign Affairs. 1996.

181.   Izadi B. Foreign Policy of the Islamic Republic of Iran // Tehran, Center. Qom Seminary Publishing, 1992.

182.   Seyfulla S. A look at the Greater Middle East [electronic source]. Available at: http://www.aftabir.com/articles/view/politics/world/c1c1223882561_the_middle_east

183.   The Middle East and the geographical position of Iran in the region, 2010. [electronic source]. Available at: http://siasatrooz.ir/vdcgty9n.ak9tn4prra.html

184.   Niakuyi S., Behmanesh H. Opposite actors in the Syrian crisis: goals and approaches // Foreign Relations Quarterly Journal, 2012.

185.   Rajabi S. Analysis of the Syria's Strategic Position in Regional and International Relations, 2012.

186.   The unique relationship between Tehran and Damascus // Special website of the Supreme Leader's Representative Office in Hajj and Pilgrimage Affairs. [electronic source]. Available at: http://hajj.ir/hadjwebui/news/wfShowOpinion.aspx?id=50812

187.   Taremi K. Analysis of Iranian national security policies towards the Middle East during the government of Mohammad Reza Pahlavi, 1969-1979 // Journal of the faculty of law and political science (University of Tehran), 2000.

188.   Kazemian M. Where will Iran go with Syria? 2013. [electronic source]. Available at: https://www.radiozamaneh.com/245551

189.   Sadat A.R. Saudi Arabia // Foundation of printing and publishing of the Ministry of Foreign Affairs. 1995.

190.   Lahouti A. United States of America and security of the Persian Gulf // Magazine of political and economic information.

191.   Homayun B. Secret relations between the United States and Saudi Arabia (weapon-oil-Iran-Iraq) // Magazine of political and economic information.

192.   Asadi S. Effective variables in Foreign Policy of Saudi Arabia // Foreign Policy Quarterly, 2011.

193.   Bazargan M. Iran's Revolution in two Movements // Tehran publisher, 1981-82.

194.   Foreign policy and international relations in the viewpoint of Imam Khomeini // Tehran: Institute for publishing works f Imam Khomeini Works, 2002.

195.   Sariolghalam M. Foreign policy of the Islamic Republic of Iran: theoretical review and coalition paradigm // Tehran: Strategic Research Center, 2000.

196.   Izadi B. On the foreign policy of the Islamic Republic of Iran // Qom: book boostan, 1992.

197. Haghighat S. Transnational responsibilities in Islamic Republic foreign Policy // Tehran: Presidential Strategic Research Center, 1997.

198. In search of the way of the words of the Imam (tenth workbook) // Tehran: Amir Kabir, 1983-1984.

199. Message from Imam on the occasion of the anniversary of the bloody Mecca incident, 1988.

200. Imam Khomeini's statement on the Shah's mission to implement colonial, economic-cultural plans, 1978.

201. Imam Khomeini's statements in among of all ambassadors, 1984.

202. Interview of Imam Khomeini with the Unita newspaper, the Organ of the communist party of Italy, 1983.

203. Ghazizadeh K. Islamic jurisprudential and political ideas of Imam Khomeini // Tehran: Presidential center of strategic studies, 1998.

204. Sotoudeh M. Imam Khomeini and theoretical foundations of foreign policy // Political science quarterly, 1999.

205. Message from Imam Khomeini on the occasion of the holy and martyrdom, 1981.

206. Meeting with the members of the Center Council of Lebanese Hezbollah, 1987.

207. Message from Imam Khomeini on the occasion of the birth and procession of Prophet Muhammad, 1980.

208. Message from Imam on the occasion of the second anniversary of the victory of the revolution, 1981.

209. Imam Khomeini's statement in a group of personnel of the Ministry of Roads & Urban Development, 1984.

210. Imam Khomeini's statements in the words of Sayyid Ali Khamenei , 1986.

211. Azghandi A. Foreign policy of the Islamic Republic of Iran // Tehran: Qumis, 2005.

212. Ostovan H. Negative balance policy in the 14th Iranian majlis, Volume 1 // Tehran: Mossadegh, 1976.

213. Mahdavi A. H. Iranian foreign policy during the Pahlavi era of 1951-1978 // Tehran: Alborz, 1994.

214. Gasiorowski M. J. American foreign policy and the Shah, translated by Fereidoun Fatemi // Tehran: Center, 1992.

215. Ramezani R. An analytical framework for foreign policy review of the Islamic Republic of Iran // Tehran: Ney, 2005.

216. Bazargan M. Instruments and problems of the first years of the revolution // Tehran: Bina, 1983.

217. Khomeini R. // Tehran: Institute for compilation and publication of Imam Khomeini's works, 1993.

218. Firouzabadi S. J. D. Structural obstacles of the regional supremacy of the Islamic Republic of Iran, encyclopedia of law and politics // Quarterly journal of faculty of law and political science, science and research branch, 2005.

219. Thirty-five-year anniversary of the Islamic Revolution. What did the eight Presidents have done for the progress of it? 2013. [electronic source]. Available at: http://www.khabaronline.ir/detail/337238/Politics/government

220. Veldani A. J. Iran and international law // Tehran: pazineh publications, 2001.

221. Ghorbani G. The role of Hafez al-Assad in the political stabilization of Syria, 2000.

222. Ettelaat newspaper. June 19, 2000.

223. Amani M. A. A study of the political relations between Syria and Iraq in the 1980s // Tehran: Ministry of foreign relations, 1995.

224. Nezhad M.B. Justice from the perspective of political current events // Political Studies and Research Institute, 2008.

226. Keyhan B. The foreign policy of Iran in the Middle East // The publishing house of the Ministry of Foreign Affairs, 2015.

www.ingramcontent.com/pod-product-compliance
Lightning Source LLC
Chambersburg PA
CBHW081657270326
41933CB00017B/3198